The Birthplace and Parentage of William Paterson. With Suggestions for Improvements On the Scottish Registers

THE

BIRTHPLACE AND PARENTAGE

OF

WILLIAM PATERSON.

EDINBURGH :
PRINTED BY BALLANTYNE AND COMPANY,
PAUL'S WORK.

THE

BIRTHPLACE AND PARENTAGE

OF

WILLIAM PATERSON,

FOUNDER OF THE BANK OF ENGLAND, AND PROJECTOR
OF THE DARIEN SCHEME:

WITH

SUGGESTIONS FOR IMPROVEMENTS ON
THE SCOTTISH REGISTERS.

BY

WILLIAM PAGAN, F.S.A., Scot.,

AUTHOR OF "ROAD REFORM," ETC.

It is deeply to be regretted that no satisfactory memorials have been
preserved of this remarkable man."— Dr ROBERT CHAMBERS.

EDINBURGH:
WILLIAM P. NIMMO.
1865.

210. g. 31.

CONTENTS.

PAGE

BIRTHPLACE AND PARENTAGE OF WILLIAM PATERSON,   1

THE SCOTTISH REGISTERS, AND THEIR IMPROVEMENT,   75

APPENDIX A.—ABRIDGMENT OF PATERSON'S LIFE,   . 103

APPENDIX B.—SASINE IN FAVOUR OF JOHN PATERSON, 118

APPENDIX C.—SASINE IN FAVOUR OF MRS BETHIA

PATERSON, ... 121

APPENDIX D.— DR CARLYLE ON TINWALD MANSE

ECONOMY, ... 124

APPENDIX E.—JOHN CUNNINGHAM AND HIS FAMILY, 125

APPENDIX F.—THE DARIEN HOUSE,   .   .   . 130

APPENDIX G.—ORIGIN OF THE NAME "PAGAN,"   . 131

BIRTHPLACE AND PARENTAGE

OF

WILLIAM PATERSON.

HAVING recently discovered in the Land Registers of
Scotland incontrovertible evidence that William Paterson, founder of the Bank of England, and projector of
the Darien colony, was the son of John Paterson, in
Skipmyre, parish of Trailflatt, now Tinwald, Dumfriesshire, I proceed to make it known in the hope of
for ever setting at rest the doubts which have been
started respecting his birthplace ; doubts which Mr Saxe
Bannister, the latest and most elaborate of Paterson's
biographers, appears to entertain, or at least has not, with
all his industry, been able in the course of his three
volumes, to clear up or dispel.* In doing so, I am well

* 1. William Paterson, the merchant, statesman, and founder of
the Bank of England; his Life and Trials, by Saxe Bannister,
M.A., formerly Attorney-General of New South Wales. Edinburgh:
W. P. Nimmo, 1858. 2. The Writings of Wm. Paterson, by the
same, 2 vols. London: Effingham Wilson, 1858.

A

assured that any fresh information respecting this most
remarkable man will be fully appreciated by all who take
an interest in those who have contributed by their
genius to the early progress, as well of England as of
Scotland, and will be appreciated, too, by the future
historian.* Seven illustrious cities, we are told, disputed
the honour of having given birth to the greatest of the
ancient poets :—

> "Smyrna, Chios, Colophon, Salamis, Rhodus, Argos, Athenæ,
>   Orbis de patriâ certat, Homere, tuâ."

Here, however, there is no claimant for Paterson's
birthplace, save the solitary farm-house of Skipmyre;
and all the more strange is it that doubts on the subject
should have entered his biographer's mind, unprepared as
he evidently was, to assert or to prove, that any other
spot in Her Majesty's dominions, or in the world, could
claim Paterson for a son.

One of the earliest printed records, relied on in
reference to such matters in Scotland, is the Statistical
Account, 1791, drawn up by the Scottish parochial
clergy, at the instance of the late Sir John Sinclair, of
Ulbster, Bart.; and there, under the head Tinwald and
Trailflatt, it is stated plainly enough :—"*Eminent men.*—
The famous Paterson, who planned the Darien scheme,
and the Bank of England, &c., was born at Skipmyre, a

---

* For the convenience of the general reader, an Abridgment of
Paterson's Life, from Dr Robert Chambers's Biographical Dictionary
will be found in Appendix A.

farm in the old parish of Trailflatt, about the year 1660. He does not seem to have been an obscure Scotsman, as a certain writer styles him. The same house gave birth to his grand-nephew, Dr James Mounsey, first physician for many years to the Empress of Russia. The widow (Mrs Alexander Mounsey) who now enjoys the farm, is sister to Dr John Rogerson, who succeeded Dr Mounsey as first physician to the Empress."

The Rev. Alexander Robison was the first minister of Tinwald after the restoration of Presbytery. He was inducted 16th March 1697, and served the cure for the long period of sixty-five years. The Rev. John Marshall succeeded him in 1762, and served till 1777. The Rev. Mr Williamson was the next incumbent, and served till 1784, when the Rev. James Lawrie, the author of the above statement, was inducted. Mr Lawrie served the cure for fifteen years till 1799, when he was succeeded by the Rev. George Greig. The fact of Paterson having been born at Skipmyre in Tinwald, was repeated in the New Statistical Account of the parish, 1834, drawn up by Mr Greig and his son and assistant, the Rev. George Greig, now minister of Kirkpatrick-Durham, in Galloway.

In making the above pointed statement, it is to be presumed that Mr Lawrie believed what he said, and that he had reliable grounds for his belief. The idea that the minister of a Scottish parish could palm on the public as matter of fact a false or even a doubtful statement is not for a moment to be credited. Paterson died in 1719, that is,

within sixty-five years of Mr Lawrie's becoming minister of
the parish ; and apart from ancient parochial records, now
unfortunately lost, but which Mr Lawrie may have seen,
there would be old persons in and about Tinwald in 1784,
and subsequently, who knew all about Paterson and his
ancestry, and from whom Mr Lawrie would have his
information. Indeed, the Mounsey branch—that is, the
descendants of the marriage between Thomas Mounsey
and the banker's elder sister Janet—was in the same farm
of Skipmyre from 1701 or earlier, partly in Mr Robison's
time, and the whole times of Mr Marshall, Mr Williamson, Mr Lawrie, and Mr Greig, down indeed till so
recently as 1844.

The widow lady, Mrs Jean Rogerson or Mounsey, the
occupant of Skipmyre farm when Mr Lawrie wrote,
(1791,) was relict of Alexander Mounsey, a grandson of
the banker's sister Janet, and her husband Thomas
Mounsey. She died on 13th May 1820, at the advanced
age of eighty-one.* The Rev. Mr Lawrie clearly enough
had access to sufficient authorities — this widowed
parishioner and relative amongst others—for the statement repecting Paterson's birthplace, and respecting the
birthplace of Dr Mounsey, a man also of celebrity, that
the same house at Skipmyre in Tinwald had given birth
to both. Had what he said and published in the end
of last century been anyways inconsistent with the truth,
many persons then alive and cognizant of the facts,

* See inscriptions on stone III., p. 22, *infra.*

would have been ready enough to come forward and contradict him.

Another thing noted by Mr Lawrie, as the quotation shews, was, that while proprietors in his parish had been frequently changing, "some farms had been rented by the same families for the space of three hundred years." Among these long leaseholders in Tinwald and Trailflatt, the Patersons may have numbered. At least, while we find them being born, and marrying, and dying, at Skipmyre, in the end of the seventeenth century, there is nothing positively to mark the period when first they settled there. The circumstance of certain families holding farms for three centuries would, we doubt not, be a matter of *tradition;* still the tradition was of that kind likely to be handed faithfully down from one generation to another; frequently to be spoken of at the farmer's ingle, and always remembered with pride. As mentioned by Mr Lawrie, the population of his small rural parish numbered only 850 souls, and the history of all the families would be intimately known, as well to each other as to the minister.

Unquestionably there was a general credence—we might almost use the word universal—in Skipmyre having had the honour of the birth. Such was accepted by Dr Robert Chambers in his "Life of Paterson," quoted in the Appendix, as well as by the "Encyclopædia Britannica," and other standard works. Indeed, as already said, there was no other claimant for it. Mr Hill Burton, however, writing

in 1852 and 1853, took a different view, and twice over
pointedly expressed his unbelief. One passage bears :—
"There is no visible authority for the statement that
Paterson was a native of the parish of Tinwald, and no
means of knowing that he was a native of Scotland."*
Another passage bears :—"The most diligent investigators
have discovered nothing about the time and place, either
of his birth or death." †

The time of birth, and time and place of death, have,
we think, been made clear enough by Mr Bannister. But
that gentleman has not attempted to meet Mr Burton's
challenge, that "there is no visible authority for the
statement that Paterson was a native of the parish of
Tinwald, and no means of knowing that he was a native
of Scotland." We undertake, however, to establish beyond
all doubt the truth of the statement in both respects,—
that Paterson was a Tinwald man and a native of Scotland.

Paterson's latter will and testament, as quoted by Mr
Bannister from the Record in Doctors' Commons, attests
the time of birth, and throws much light on the banker's
relatives and connexions.   That most interesting document runs as follows :—

"I William Paterson, of the city of Westminster,
Esquire, being in good health of body and mind, for
which I most humbly thank and praise Almighty God,

* Narratives from Criminal Trials in Scotland, vol. i., p. 105.
London, 1852.

† The History of Scotland from 1689 to 1748, vol. i., p. 284.
London, 1853.

the ever blessed Maker and Preserver of all, do make this my last will and testament. After my debts paid, I give to Elizabeth, my daughter-in-law, only child to my first wife, Mrs Elizabeth Turner, relict to the late Mr Thomas Bridge, minister of the gospel in Boston, in New England, fifteen hundred pounds. 2d, I give to my eldest daughter-in-law, Anne, by my second wife, Mrs Hannah Kemp, married to Mr Samuel South, six hundred pounds. 3d, I give to my second daughter-in-law Mary, married to Mr Mark Holman, six hundred pounds. 4th, I give to my two other daughters-in-law, Hannah and Elizabeth Kemp, eight hundred pounds each. 5th, I give to Jane Kemp, relict of the late Mr James Kemp, my son-in-law, three hundred pounds. 6th, I give to William Mounsey, eldest son of my late sister Janet, two hundred pounds. 7th, I give to the two daughters of my said late sister Janet, Elizabeth and Janet, two hundred pounds each. 8th, I give to John Mounsey, younger son of my said late sister Janet, four hundred pounds. 9th, I give to my only sister Elizabeth, married to John Paterson, younger of Kinharvey, in the stewartry of Kirkcudbright, eight hundred pounds. 10th, I give the surplus of my estate, if, after payment of my debts, any such shall be, to be equally divided among the said persons, legatees, in proportion to every person's sum hereby bequeathed; all which sums above given, amounting to six thousand and four hundred pounds, I appoint to be paid by my executor here immediately afternamed. I do hereby appoint my good friend, Mr Paul Daranda, of London, merchant, to whom I and my family are under very great obligations, sole executor of this my last will ; and I do allow him, as my sole executor, one thousand pounds for his care therein, over his expenses with relation hereto. Lastly, I revoke all other wills by me heretofore made. In witness whereof, I have hereto subscribed my name and put my seal, at Westminster, this first day of July 1718, in the sixtieth year and third month of my age.— WILLIAM PATERSON.   Witnesses : Ed. Bagshawe, Hen. Dollan, John Butler."

On the 3d July 1718, the testator certified the making of this will "at the Ship Tavern, without Temple Bar, about four in the afternoon." " Proved in Doctors' Commons, 22d January 1719, o.s."*

In the above important document—the closing chapter of the chequered life of this distinguished individual—a great flood of light is thrown upon his position, his pecuniary circumstances, and his collateral relations. He therein describes himself as of the City of Westminster—comfortably seated there in Queen's Square, as Mr Bannister has ascertained,—as being sixty years and a quarter old, so making April 1658 the period of his birth,—as bequeathing legacies to the amount of £7400, (including that to his executor,) besides a probable surplus to be similarly divided,—all, we may suppose, the reversion of

* Life of Paterson, p. 427.

the parliamentary grant of £18,241, 10s. 10⅔d., made him in 1715, on account of his public services, immediately after the accession of George *First*. The will further describes him as having been twice married, as having had a sister Janet, who left four children—William, Elizabeth, Janet, and John Mounsey; and as then having an only sister, Elizabeth, married to John Paterson, younger, of Kinharvey, in the stewartry of Kirkcudbright.

Mr Bannister also quotes a letter, (Writings, vol. i., p. cxxvi.,) addressed by Paterson to Earl Stanhope, and preserved in the State-Paper Office, (domestic,) dated "Westminster, 8th December 1718." That was within six or seven weeks of his death, which of course happened previous to the proving of the will in Doctors' Commons, on 22d January 1719, o.s. Mr Bannister further states the exact day of death as 22d January, and refers to the historical register as his voucher. The fair inference, then, is, that if removed from Queen Square, autumn 1718, Paterson had found a dwelling in another part of the same city, (Westminster,) and died there in January following.

Respecting Paterson's parentage and place of birth, however, Mr Bannister, and all others who had written of him, were equally in the dark. None of them could name either his father or his mother, and none of them had any knowledge of his birthplace, further than that asserted by the Rev. Mr Lawrie, in the Statistical Account. Mr Bannister, as he states, had been at great pains in searching old records, but there being none extant for Tinwald or Trailflatt parish in the seventeenth century, when the birth took place, he arrived at the conclusion that the birth at Skipmyre could not be relied on as more than a mere tradition. Mr Bannister's words are :—"A strong tradition in Dumfriesshire fixes his birth in that county; and although no baptismal registry exists for the parish where it has long been popularly held he was born, the minister of that parish, in the last century, gave in a formal statistical report* about it, that the farm of Skipmyre, in Trailflatt, anciently annexed to Tinwald, as the residence of Paterson's father and mother, where he was born. The same farm has for generations been pointed out as the birthplace of ' the founder of the Bank of England;' and the house itself was pulled down within a few years only." †

Further on, (p. 431,) Mr Bannister speaks of Paterson's "native Dumfries hills ;" and at another place the same gentleman says :—"Nor was a doubt ever raised till recently as to his birthplace in Scotland. Tradition is uniform on this head; and the honour of being his birthplace was long claimed for Lochmaben, [should be Skipmyre,] in Tinwald, in Dumfriesshire, with which county many associations belonging to him are con-

---

* Sir John Sinclair's Statistical Account of Scotland, vol. i., p. 165. † Bannister's Life, p. 35.

nected. Topographical works of repute support the claim," &c. *

Elsewhere, in speaking of Paterson's election for the Dumfries burghs, to the first united Parliament in 1708, (but upon a double return, and where he did not get the seat,) Mr Bannister ("Life," p. 32) draws the inference that Paterson "was born in Scotland"—an inference he supports by reference to an acknowledgment by the directors of the Darien Company, all Scotchmen, of the services rendered by Paterson to his "native country." † Whether Mr Bannister was persuaded in his own mind of the birthplace being at Skipmyre, or merely at some place in Scotland, does not appear; and certainly he has filled up three goodly volumes without meeting the challenge hazarded some years before, in the works of Mr Hill Burton, already alluded to, of there being "no visible authority for the statement that Paterson was a native of the parish of Tinwald, and no means of knowing that he was a native of Scotland."

The circumstance of Mr Bannister's having left unsettled these most interesting points—the birthplace and parentage of Paterson—was exceedingly unsatisfactory, and especially so to the many who had been taught to believe in his Dumfriesshire origin. For myself, I was fully impressed with the truth of the Statistical Account. I had, indeed, evidence—traditionary evidence—to the same

* Bannister's Biographical Introduction to Paterson's Writings, vol. i., p. xx.   † Ibid., p. xix.

effect, and which a judge or jury would receive in corroboration. When apprenticed in Dumfries, between 1817 and 1822, with the late Mr William Thomson, sheriff-clerk of Dumfriesshire, and provost of Dumfries, the agent for Charles, Marquis of Queensberry, then proprietor of the barony of Tinwald, including the farm of Skipmyre, I was several times in that and the adjoining parishes of Torthorwald, Lochmaben, and Mousewald, with Mr Thomson and his nephew, the late Mr William Pagan, of Curriestanes, in the stewartry of Kirkcudbright, (my father,) inspecting and valuing farms for Lord Queensberry; and in passing they spoke of Skipmyre farm-house as the birthplace of Paterson, the founder of the Bank of England. Mr Thomson was born in Torthorwald parish, in the immediate vicinity of Skipmyre, about 1770, and my father in Mouswald parish, also near by. Both of them were acquainted with persons and places connected with those localities. Mr Thomson's father and grandfather (both Torthorwald men) would know the banker's father and his family—probably the banker himself, who died, as we have seen, in 1719; that is, just fifty-one years before Mr Thomson's birth. At any rate, both Mr Thomson and my father knew the Mounsey branch of the family, who were still in possession of the same farm of Skipmyre that had accrued to them from the banker's father. They would also know of the Patersons of Kinharvey, with whom a sister of the banker intermarried, as mentioned in his will, and who was alive in 1740. For myself, then, I had no manner of doubt that Skipmyre was the birthplace; and were it at all necessary, I am certain evidence of a similar character, and to the like effect, could yet be found in the district respecting the eminent man after whom we are here inquiring.

I should notice also that in one of the above-mentioned years, I was at the old house of Skipmyre, the very birthplace, not on a business or genealogical or archæological errand, but simply on a small hare-hunting excursion.* The Mounsey of the day, a descendant of the banker's sister Janet, asked me in, and a grateful recollection of his hospitality on the occasion is still on my mind. But instead of attempting a description of the building, I prefer quoting an account of it by a learned gentleman, in the *Edinburgh Review* of January 1862. In reviewing Mr Bannister's volumes, so often already referred to, along with the three relative undernoted works,† the reviewer said :—"William Paterson was born

---

* In the early part of this century, Dumfrieshire was quite a sporting country, and the parish of Tinwald (so often mentioned) afforded a course—the well-known Tinwald downs—for the Dumfries races. The course is now obliterated, covered with luxuriant white and green crops, and the gaiety and excitement which for long attached to that popular institution—the "southern meeting," are, alas! only matter of history.

† The Darien Papers, 1695–1700: printed by the Bannatyne Club. Edinburgh, 1849. 2. Darien; or, the Merchant Prince, by the author of "The Crescent and the Cross." And 3. Isthmus of Darien Ship Canal, by Dr Cullen, 1853.

in the spring of 1655, [should be 1658;] and a tradition
so constant, as to leave no reasonable ground for scepti-
cism, fixes on the farm-house of Skipmyre, in the parish
of Tinwald, Dumfriesshire, as the place of his birth. It
is, or rather was, (for it has been pulled down lately,)
a solitary farm-house on the crest of a hill, as you rise
from Lochmaben, in the vale of Annan, on the way to
Dumfries. It may have been the residence of a small
proprietor two centuries ago; and although Paterson's
father held it merely as a tenant, it probably was superior to the ordinary farm-houses in the district, as the
family is said to have removed, [this is a mistake,] when
Paterson was a child, to Kinharvey, near Newabbey,
which is still a gentleman's seat. . . . There can be
no question, from the position of his numerous relatives,
that Paterson belonged to that extensive class in Scotland, which hangs between the farmers and the minor
gentry. . . . His parents certainly were not wealthy,
but in addition to his farm, it is said that his father
possessed a small estate in the neighbourhood called
Craigield."

Having it impressed on my mind, from the circumstances above mentioned, that Paterson belonged to
Skipmyre, in Dumfriesshire, and was also connected
with the property or family of Kinharvey, in Newabbey
parish, across the Nith,—(and indeed owing my own birth
to the parish of Dumfries, which adjoins Tinwald, and my
upbringing to the parish of Troqueer in the stewartry,

which borders on Newabbey)—I felt concerned alike on local and on historical grounds, that Paterson's latest and fullest biographer had not cleared up the birthplace and parentage, but had left the question of the former in doubt, and the latter wholly unsolved. It was, therefore, with no little interest, in recently searching, (but for another purpose altogether,) one of the old registers of Scotland—the Minute-Book (abbreviate) of the Particular Register of Sasines, kept at Dumfries for the county of Dumfries, and stewartry of Kirkcudbright, that I noticed in it, in *juxtaposition*, the names of Paterson of Kinharvey, and Paterson of Skipmyre. The entry was in these terms :—"Dumfries, 31st May 1701, betwixt three and four hours in the afternoon, produced by Mr Robert Edgar, writer, yre, sasine in favor of John Patersone, eldest lawful son to John Patersone of Kinharvie, in ye lands of Kinharvie *alias* Clocklowie,—*Item*, Sasine in favour of Bethia Patersone, spous to ye said John Patersone, lawful daughter to John Patersone, Skipmyre, in ane yearly a rent of fourtie pounds Scots, furth of ye saids lands after his decease."

It crossed my mind on the instant that the sasines mentioned in the above entry in the county register might aid in clearing up Paterson's genealogy ; and on referring at my leisure to the volume where full copies of the minuted deeds are engrossed, it appeared to me that the contents of that register, in conjunction with Paterson's deed of settlement above quoted, made it clear as noon-

day, that John Paterson and Bethia Paterson in Skipmyre, spouses, were the father and mother of the banker,
and that the Rev. Mr Lawrie in his statistical account
had rightly set down Skipmyre as the birthplace. I found
that both sasines proceeded on one and the same deed,
being a contract of marriage between John Paterson,
younger, and Bethia Paterson—who was no other than
the Elizabeth, sister of the banker, the same lady to
whom in his will he left £800. His bequest to her was
in these words :—"9th, I give to my only (surviving)
sister Elizabeth, married to John Paterson, younger, of
Kinharvey, in the stewartry of Kirkcudbright, eight hundred pounds." The contract of marriage itself is not to be
found, and has possibly long ago perished, but the recital
of it in the sasines is full and clear. The record of the
two sasines may be seen in Her Majesty's General Register
House, Edinburgh ; and as all important in this question,
full length copies of them are given in the Appendix.
Their import may be stated in few words :—

1. The sasine in favour of John Paterson, the younger,[*]
bears that on 22d April 1701, in the thirteenth year of
King William's reign, in presence of a notary and witnesses, John Paterson of Kinharvey, appeared on the
lands of Kinharvey; also John Paterson, his eldest lawful son, the latter having in his hands a contract of
marriage, past and ended betwixt him, with consent of
his said father, and Bethia Paterson, lawful daughter to

* Appendix B.

John Paterson in Skipmyre, with consent of her father, of date 19th March last past. By which contract, in contemplation of the marriage then contracted and after solemnised betwixt the said parties, the said John Paterson, elder, obliged himself to infeft and seize the said John Paterson, his son, and his heirs and successors, heritably and irredeemably, in his forty-shilling land of Kinharvey or Clocklowie, with houses, &c., lying within the parish of Newabbey, and stewartry of Kirkcudbright —reserving to himself and Margaret Affleck, his spouse and survivor, their liferent of the lands during their lifetime: thereupon, after the accustomed ceremonies observed for ages in infeftments according to the feudal system in Scotland, (but which ceremonies, sasines and all, are now abolished,)—the father gave infeftment of his lands to his son, reserving the father and mother's liferent, as above mentioned. These things were done, time and place above mentioned, before Thomas Muncie (*anglicé* Mounsey) in Skipmyre, James Paterson in Cullencleugh, James Paterson, second lawful son to John Paterson, elder, (of Kinharvey,) and William Muncie, son to said Thomas Muncie.

2. The sasine in favour of Bethia Paterson,* bears that on the same day, and year, and king's reign, John Paterson, younger, and Bethia Paterson, spouses, appeared on the lands of Kinharvey—the husband having and holding in his hands the above-mentioned contract of marriage,

---

* Appendix C.

B

made and ended, &c., of date 19th March last past. By
which contract the said John Paterson, younger, bound
himself to infeft his wife in an yearly annuity of forty
pounds Scots money, payable by equal portions at Whitsunday and Martinmas, to be lifted forth of the forty
shilling lands of Kinharvey or Clocklowie, &c., lying
within the parish of Newabbey, and stewartry of Kirkcudbright. Then follows a *proviso*, that the said annuity should
be without prejudice to " ane farther additional liferent
annuity and provision corresponding and suitable to the
moveable goods, gear, and others which were thereby
assigned," (but the particulars of the assignation not copied
into the sasine,) "in favour of him and his said spouse by
the said John Patersone in Skipmyre, and which shall
accress to them at his decease, under reservation of
Bethia Patersone, spouse to the said John Patersone, elder,
her just third part and share thereof, whilk additional
liferent provisions accordingly the said John Patersone
stands bound and obliged,* and to grant in favour of his
said spouse all writs and securities thereupon for her
said liferent in case of her survivance." Thereupon, the
husband, Kinharvey the younger, gave infeftment to his
said spouse, Bethia, daughter of Skipmyre, of the foresaid lands in security of the said forty pounds yearly of
annuity. These things were done, time and place above

---

* A written obligation by John of Skipmyre, in favour of Bethia
Paterson, his wife, seems here referred to—probably a contract of
marriage between them—but of such deed I have not been able to
find any trace.

mentioned, and before the same four witnesses as in the husband's own sasine,—Thomas Muncie in Skipmyre, and William Muncie his son, and James Paterson, second son to John Paterson, elder, (of Kinharvey,) being, as before, of the number of the witnesses.

Marriage settlements, like latter wills and testaments, frequently disclose many genealogical particulars of the parties concerned; and in the recital now given of the marriage contract between Paterson the younger and his wife Bethia we have information of a reliable character, —probably not elsewhere extant. The Church of Scotland, from its earliest institution, had established parochial registers over all Scotland, of births, marriages, and deaths; but in the unsettled state of the country during the seventeenth century—particularly in the Covenanting distractions which long overshadowed the south and west of Scotland—entries of births, marriages, and deaths would not be regularly made, and when made, the registers would frequently perish. In Tinwald, for instance, the earliest birth, marriage, and death register to be found, commences after the middle of the eighteenth century, and so throws no light on the parish births and marriages in the preceding century.

As I read those two sasines, now fortunately brought to light, we have the following points established:— 1. That John Paterson of Kinharvey, (1701,) and Margaret Affleck his spouse, had an eldest lawful son, John Paterson, younger. 2. That John Paterson, in Skipmyre, and

Bethia Paterson, his wife, had a daughter, Bethia. 3. That Kinharvey the younger and this daughter were married on 19th March 1701; and 4. That the immediate family connexions, Thomas Muncie, *anglicé* Mounsey, in Skipmyre, and William, son of Thomas Muncie, were of the chosen witnesses. Then looking to Paterson's will of 1718, recognising Kinharvey the younger's wife as his sister, we can have no hesitation in concluding that John Paterson in Skipmyre, and Bethia Paterson his wife, were father and mother, both of William the banker, and of his sister Elizabeth, Mrs Paterson. If we are right in this, then is the question of Paterson's parentage for ever solved, and solved quite in conformity with the received opinion on the subject.

According to a genealogical tree recently framed by the Mounsey branch of the family, and communicated to me by one of its members, Mr George Graham, engineer of the Caledonian Railway Company, Glasgow, Paterson's grandfather was in Skipmyre about 1600, and was therein followed by the father, now ascertained to be John Paterson. Of him the first written record I have yet discovered, is an entry of date 10th October 1697, in the discipline records of the Kirk-Session of Tinwald—found upon a search therein obligingly made for me by the Rev. James Vallance, present minister of the parish. That entry bears :—"Tinwald, Octr. 10, 1697. *Inter alia*, this day Thomas Johnstone, servant to John Paterson, in Skipmyre, was declared guilty," &c. The next and only other written record of Skipmyre's existence *yet* known—for others, his leases of Skipmyre, for instance, may hereafter cast up—is the narrative of his daughter Bethia or Elizabeth's contract of marriage, 1701, found in the above-mentioned sasines as recorded in the Particular Register at Dumfries, and now preserved in Her Majesty's General Register House, Edinburgh.

I learned, however, in corresponding with the Rev. Mr Vallance, that the Patersons had a burying-place in the graveyard of the old parish of Trailflatt, marked by a group of tombstones still extant ; and at my request Mr Vallance kindly went and examined and deciphered them. He has furnished me with copies of the following most interesting inscriptions legible on the stones, and which of themselves establish the fact of the Patersons having been in Skipmyre in the seventeenth century, if not earlier, down to a recent date. These are the inscriptions, giving precedence in the order of their dates :—

I.

"In memory of Margaret Wilkin, spouse to James Paterson in Skipmyre, who died February 1694; also James Paterson in Skipmyre, who died May 29, 1722, aged 101 years; also Adam Paterson his son, who died May 29, 1737, aged 71 years. W. G."

II.

"Here lyes James Paterson, son to John Paterson in

Skepmire, who deceased the 5th of April 1694 ; and John & William Paterson.

"Here lyes the corpse of John Mounsey in Shieldhill, son to William Mounsey in Skipmyre, who departed this life the 2d of Aprill 1751, aged 23 years. *Memento mori.*"

III.

"In memory of John Paterson in Skipmyre, who died February 7th, 1694.

"Also William Mounsey in Skipmire, who died April 23, 1751, aged 63 years ; also Margret Rogerson his spouse, who died Nov. 19, 1760, aged 65 years.

" Also Alexr. Mounsey their son, who died July 31, 1785, aged 56 years ; also Jean Rogerson his spouse, who died May 3, 1820, aged 81 years ; also Samuel Mounsey their son, who died June 9, 1797, aged 26 years.

" Also William, son to the said William Mounsey, who died Jan. 23, 1793, aged 60 years.

"Also William, son to the said Alexr. Mounsey, who died 22 Decr. 1829, aged 67."

IV.

"Here lyes Jannet Pattersone, lait spouse to Thomas Munsie, merchand, Skipmyre, who died the 26 day of Novr. 1698 ; and here lyes T. M. and A. M. their children.

"Here lyeth the body of Thomas Monsie in Skipmyre, who departed this life, Augt. the 6th, 1711, aged 55 years; also here lyeth the body of Mary Steell, spouse to Thomas Mounsie, who departed this life the 23d of May 1747, aged 63 years.

"In memory of Jean White, spouse to James Mounsey in Skipmyre, who died June 21, 1820, aged 43 years; also James their son, who died Augt. 6, 1812, aged 2 years; also William their son, who died 31 March 1825, aged 14 years; also James their son, who died 2 June 1825, aged 12 years; also the said James Mounsey, who died 10 March 1635, aged 55 years. Also interred here, John Mounsey, M.D. his son, who died in Manchester, 26 October 1837, aged 29 years."

Not to have any mistake in the matter, I made a pilgrimage to the Trailflatt burying-ground, on August 12, 1864, with Mr Vallance for my guide, and verified on the spot the correctness of the copies, by comparing them with the carved inscriptions on the tombstones. The burying-ground is romantically situated on the eastern side of the Pendicle hill of Trailflatt—part of the Tinwald and Torthorwald range—and immediately be-north the farm-house and steading of Bankhead, on the estate of Tinwald, (Skipmyre included,) now the property of Captain Morden Carthew Yorston, of Craigenvey. The distance is about two miles from Skipmyre farm-house, and much the same from the ancient royal burgh of Lochmaben. The Paterson stones, as they are entitled to be called, are of the red sandstone, which is plentiful in the district ; their size about six feet by three, with six stone supports to each. Nos. II. and IV. appeared most ancient in fabric, but the whole of them are in admirable keeping. Not many years ago, as we were informed, the stones had been set up anew by the pious care of a connexion of the family, and some fresh stone supports supplied, but the carvings not interfered with. The same burying-ground contains fifty or sixty monuments or monumental stones belonging to other families of old Trailflatt—some ancient, some modern— all of them in wonderfully good order, and testifying to the care and veneration with which memorials to deceased relatives are preserved in the south of Scotland.* A number of families still bury in this ancient cemetery, and assuredly a more alluring place of repose for the ashes of mortal man is rarely to be met with :—

> [" Perhaps in this neglected spot is laid
>   Some heart once pregnant with celestial fire ;
>   Hands that the rod of empire might have sway'd,
>   Or waked to ecstacy the living lyre."

The burying-ground also contains all that remains of the church of Trailflatt—a ruin mostly of rubble or un- dressed stones. One of the gables and parts of the side walls still mark the size of the building. There is one

---

* The old churchyard of Dumfries, now specially signalised as the depository of the ashes of Burns, and as containing the mausoleum to his memory, has long been renowned for its copious and much admired collection of monumental stones to departed worth.

window extant, but all trace of doorway is obliterated —at least hidden by, rubbish—till cleared by some investigating archæologist. The *coup-d'œil* would make a good photographic picture,—embracing tombstones, church walls, enclosing hedge and trees, and hill-side. We know not at what precise period stated service was discontinued in Trailflatt Church. But according to an old (and solitary) volume of the Kirk-Session records, shewn me by Mr Vallance, worship was performed at Trailflatt and Tinwald churches alternately, down at least to 1697. The record of that year bears the following :— "At Tinwald, August 29, 1697.—*Post preces sederunt*, the Minister and Elders, excepting Alex. Clesby, who is absent. *Inter alia*, as also the Session considering how greatly God is dishonoured by the profanation of His day by those on this side of the parish, when there is a sermon in Trailflatt, and by those on the other side of the parish when sermon is here,—Therefore the Session thinks fit to give public warning, that whosoever shall· be found unnecessarily to stay from any of the said kirks shall be proceeded against as profaning the Lord's day."

Another Kirk-Session minute bears :—" At Tinwald Kirk, July 21,1698.—*Sederunt*, Minister and Elders. *Inter alia*, John Henderson being called but not compearing, Thomas Munsey (elder, and brother-in-law of the banker) is appointed to send notice to Mr Steel (minister of Lochmaben, and whose sister Munsey married for his second

wife,, and desire him to cite him (Henderson) to appear
against Sabbath-come-fortnight at the Kirk of Trail-
flat," &c.*

Skipmyre farm, as already said, was in Trailflatt parish,
the farm-house being less than two miles from the
church; and within its now venerable walls, we can
readily believe that the infant banker, born in 1658, was
baptised publicly according to the custom of the period—
a custom, indeed, still continued in many of our Scottish
congregations. At least no argument need be offered to
satisfy unprejudiced individuals that to this same Trailflatt church Paterson would be statedly taken in early life
to join in the worship of his God.

The above " testimony of the rocks," or at least of the
Trailflatt tombstones, was entirely missed by Mr Bannister.
The name of the banker's sister Janet, married to Thomas

---

* The following entry in the Kirk-Session record of March 28,
1700, indicates the reality, and what would now be called the
severity of church discipline in Tinwald and Trailflatt as then
applied to erring brethren : — " Tinwald, March 28, 1700—
Sederunt, Ministers and Elders.—Robert Richardson (who had
confessed a breach of the seventh commandment,) appearing this
day in the public place of repentance, and being called down to
the body of the congregation, and ordered to take the sackcloth
about him q[t] he had let fall from him, he instantly with contempt
went out of the church; and the Session considering that his
conduct in public was not edifying, but rather gave them renewed
scandal, they appointed the minister to converse with him in
private, in order to bring him to a sense of his sin and offensive
carriage ; and if he judged it would be edifying y[t] he order him to
appear again before the congregation the next Sabbath."

Mounsey, stands in the stone obituary of 1698, followed by that of her husband in 1711. To these have been added the names of numerous descendants of that marriage, now all mixed with the kindred dust of the Patersons. It may be taken for granted that John Paterson, father of the banker, who had his son in 1658 and was alive in 1701, was a descendant of one of the Patersons mentioned on stones I. and II. His father might be John Paterson, who died in February 1694, or he might be James Paterson, whose life was prolonged to one hundred and one years, and died in 1722. But it is not for one writing in 1864, at least without further materials, to determine the question. Suffice it to say, that there were Paterson families in Skipmyre in the seventeenth century, stretching back to an early part of it, and whose tombstones and other records make no mention of their having belonged to any other parish than this same Trailflatt; all, indeed, tending to strengthen the statistical account that the father of the banker was in Skipmyre at the time of his son's birth in 1658. The plentifulness of the Patersons, on the then small farm of Skipmyre, possibly led the youthful Paterson to leave the place—to leave Scotland—and seek that wider sphere of honour and emolument to which his genius and persever-ance carried him in other lands.

Whatever room there may be for argument respecting the great-grandfather and grandfather's names, doubt there can be none, that John Paterson in Skipmyre, men-

tioned in the Session record of 1697, and in the marriage-
contract of 1701, and Bethia Paterson, his wife, were the
parents of the banker. Both father and mother were
alive at their daughter's marriage to Kinharvey, in 1701.
. Neither being named in their son's will of 1718, we may
presume that both had predeceased him. Next to a
certainty the father and mother would be interred in the
family ground at Trailflatt, and have a stone to mark
their graves. But such does not seem now in existence;
there is neither parochial register, nor monumental relic to
attest the dates of their deaths. Indeed, after the lapse
of more than a century and a half, the disappearance of
a stone through its crumbling into dust, or through
Father Time's other chances and changes, is not to be
wondered at. Marvellous rather is it that the five stones
above particularised and the inscriptions on them—one
well on to two centuries old—should have remained
extant to tell at this distant day of those humble individuals, whose names they were designed to keep in
remembrance. Some special providential care had been
over them all that long period—a spell such as is said to
guard the grave of Shakespeare :—

> " Good friend, for Jesus' sake forbear,
>   To dig the dust enclosed here.
>   Bless'd be the man who spares these stones ;
>   And cursed be he who moves my bones."

Rumour has sometimes said that Paterson's remains
were brought down to Scotland, and interred in New-

abbey, where the Kinharvey Patersons lie, or in Trailflatt where the Skipmyre Patersons lie. If in Scotland at all—a thing not likely at the period (1719)— Trailflatt would be the place, but of which no visible trace or even probable tradition is to be found. Had the body of a man so distinguished in his country's history been brought all the way from Westminster to Dumfries, when the transit would be full of difficulties, and its time and expense of serious magnitude, the fact would have been attested by one of those Trailflatt tombstones to which the family were evidently partial; and moreover, would not have been forgotten in the history and traditions of the county and district. Instead of Newabbey or Trail- flatt, Paterson, if he thought of a resting-place for him- self at all, was more likely to choose the ground of one or other of the English families with whom he connected himself by his two marriages, and whom, as testified by liberal provisions to them in his will, he held in fond remembrance. Not a doubt, some of the burial registers in Westminster or London will contain a record of his interment as having been made there in January or February 1719.

Paradoxical as it may seem to seek evidence of a birth in a death register or on a tombstone, the latter, as we have already seen, has thrown considerable light on the Paterson genealogy—and specially on the family having been localised at Skipmyre in the seventeenth century. The Mounsey branch of the family appears clearly enough on the tombstones.

Thomas Mounsey had settled at Skipmyre, with his
father-in-law, previous to his first wife's (Janet Paterson)
death in 1698,—indeed, as we have seen in the Kirk-Session
records, he had then been preferred as a man of standing in the parish, to the office of parochial elder,—and in
Skipmyre he continued down to his own death. He was
residing there in 1701, when a witness to the sasine of
his sister-in-law, Mrs Paterson, over Kinharvey, and at
Skipmyre was born his son Dr James Mounsey, the
Russian physician, the only child of Mounsey's second
marriage with Mary Steel, already mentioned.

The father and mother having been alive at the time of
Kinharvey's marriage with their daughter in 1701, the
marriage-contract, could it be got, would possibly have
the name of the banker at it as a witness—it being customary in matrimonial transactions to assemble the near
relatives, and take them as witnesses to the marriage
settlements. By that time Paterson's principal works
were achieved—the bank of England had been established
in 1694, and from the unfortunate Darien expedition,
which occupied 1698 and 1699, he had previously returned
humiliated enough. In 1700 and 1701 his mind and pen
were employed on various important financial papers
which Mr Bannister has quoted or adverted to in his
volumes.

Speaking of the parents, of whose names or whose where-
abouts Mr Bannister confessedly knew nothing, that gentleman says their condition "was that of the wealthier

tenants of the period; * and his father appears to have also possessed lands of his own at some distance from the farm held on lease."—" Life," p. 36. For all this no authority is given, and the *locus* of the lands is not mentioned. The writer in the *Edinburgh Review* named them " Craigield," while the Rev. George Greig, now at Kirkpatrick-Durham, whose name is conjoined with that of his deceased father in the new statistical account of Tinwald, makes the name " Craigshiells " in Kirkmichael parish, adjoining Tinwald. In the hope of discovering something of those lands, and of the father in connexion with them, I searched the Particular Register of Sasines already alluded to, (Dumfries and Kirkcudbright,) from its institution in 1617 downwards for a century or more, but without finding any John Paterson in Skipmyre, mentioned as a proprietor or seller of lands, or as a party or witness to any infeftment. I made a similar unavailing search in the General Register of Sasines at Edinburgh, for nearly the same period, with an equally fruitless result. Neither saw I anything of a contract of marriage, as between John, of Skipmyre, and Bethia—though from the wording of their daughter's contract

* According to the Queensberry Rental of 1760—half a century and more after the time of Paterson's father and mother here alluded to—matters stood thus :—Hunterhouse farm and half of Skipmyre, £55; Skipmyre, the other half, (supposed Paterson's,) £29, 10s. On this modest rental the father and mother would scarcely rank among the " wealthier tenants of the period." On the contrary, (and no disparagement,) " their haddin would be sma' ! "

with Kinharvey, younger, such may have been. The name of William the banker nowhere appeared in the General or Particular Registers searched by me.

I should note, however, that no minute-book or abbreviate of the above-mentioned particular Landed Register 1617-71 appears to have been made up. My search was, therefore, so far in the register of full length copies, but where unhappily there are distressing blanks from March 1620 to February 1624 and from 1660 to 1671. I am aware that Mr George Brown Robertson, deputy-keeper of the records, and to whom in my searches I have more than once been indebted, has sought after the missing volumes, but in vain. Their loss is all the greater, that there is no minute-book of that period—no abridgment to indicate the contents of the register for the fifteen years of the missing volumes. The minute-book of the Dumfries and Kirkcudbright Registers commences in 1671, from which date down to the present day, both registers and minute-book are continuous and correct.

The minute-book of the General Register of Sasines which I searched, 1617-1700, appeared very vague in numerous instances and not to be relied on. A correct minute-book (or abbreviate) of that register, for the period referred to, ought to be made up. Till such be provided, a search in the full-length volumes is essential, where the search is to be thorough and complete. I must confess, however, that what with decayed paper, faded ink, contracted words, antiquated spellings, law Latin deeds, and cramped clerking, a search in ancient records whether general or particular, is a work of much labour but uncertain success. Possibly some more close and acute observer may yet light on a Paterson deed missed by me. Of Paterson names, however, both in the land registers and in the registers of births, marriages, and deaths, a good many appeared in Dumfriesshire and Galloway—the name being a prevailing one, and "John" Paterson the most frequent, but none of them Paterson in Skipmyre.

My search was equally fruitless in the Abbreviated Retours—(1.) Of the services of heirs in special to lands, (2.) of heirs in general to persons, (3.) of tutors to pupils or imbeciles, (4.) of old extent or value of lands, and (5.) of quinquennial possession of lands, 1560-1700. I found, among the General Retours—"8671. April 25, 1661—Joannes Patersone hæres Davidis Patersone incolæ in Nether Shiells, avi." This, however, did not apply to Paterson in Skipmyre.

Those Abbreviated Retours, though filling three ponderous volumes, folio, with double columns, were easily searched, being printed with indices of persons and places, and, moreover, being accessible at the county towns. The retours were so laid open under authority of a Royal Commission in 1806, appointed upon an address from the House of Commons; and the task, plainly a most laborious one, embracing a period of one hundred and forty

C

years, 1560-1700, was accomplished and the work published so early as 1811, under the superintendence of Mr Thomas Thomson. Printed abbreviates of the old sasine minute-books, commencing 1617, with indices of persons and places, would be of great public advantage. The improvement of the Scottish registers is urged by me in my separate remarks at the conclusion of this birthplace and parentage, and to which I beg to refer. .

The capital contributed to Paterson's great Darien scheme (1698,) and nearly all from Scotland, amounted to £400,000 sterling. Of that so much as £11,600 was from the district of his birth, as appears by the following Dumfriesshire and Galloway list, kindly supplied to me by Mr William M'Dowall, of the *Dumfries Standard :—*

William, Earl of Annandale, £1000; John Corsbie and James Coulter, merchants in Dumfries, £500; William Charters, Sheriff-Depute of Dumfries, £300; John Corbet, merchant in Dumfries, £200; Robert Corbet, merchant in Dumfries, £100; John Crosbie, merchant in Dumfries, £100; William Carruthers, of Whitecroft, £100; the Town of Dumfries, £500; Henrietta Dalyell, Lady Glenae, £200; Mrs Agnes Dalyell, daughter to the deceased Sir Robert Dalyell of Glenae, Baronet, £200; William Elliot of Borthwickhall, £200; William Ferguson, brother-german to Mr Alexander Ferguson of Isle, advocate, £100; Matthew Harestains of Craigs, £200; Patrick Heron of Kerochtrie, £200; Janet Home, Lady Eccles, £100; Andrew Heron of Bergally, £100; Sir Alexander Jardin of Applegirth, £400; Robert Johnstoun and John Reid, merchants in Dumfries, £400; Alexander Johnstoun of Edshieshiels, £400; Robert Johnstoun, late Provost of Dumfries, £400; John Irving, son to John Irving of Drumcottron, £200;

John Irving, son to John Irving, present Provost of Dumfries, £200; Thomas Irving, merchant in Dumfries, £200; Thomas Kinkaid, son to Thomas Kinkaid of Achinreogh, £500; John Lanrick, writer in Dumfries, £100; Robert Laurie, younger of Maxwelltown, £100; John Maxwell of Middlebie, £300; John Maxwell of Barncleugh, £200; Robert Maxwell of Garnsalloch, £200; William Mackgie of Balmaghie, £200; James Maxwell, eldest son of John Maxwell of Barncleugh, £100; His Grace the Duke of Queensberry, £3000; John Sharp of Hoddom, £600;— in all £11,600.

Two of the subscriptions were from the ladies of Glenae, under whom Paterson's father farmed Skipmyre, then part of the Glenae estate. To these ladies, as well as to many other of the subscribers, Paterson would be personally known. It was, indeed, the public confidence in his genius and sagacity that led to the formation of the scheme, and induced the immense pecuniary support that was accorded to it.

Dr Alexander Carlyle of Inveresk, whose interesting autobiography, edited by Mr Hill Burton, was lately published, having been a grandson of the Rev. Alexander Robison, minister of Tinwald and Trailflatt, already mentioned, we refer to that work in case it might throw light on Paterson. Dr Carlyle records several visits paid by him to his grandfather, but makes no allusion to Paterson, or the state affairs in which he had been concerned. Carlyle was born in 1722, being four years after Paterson's death.*

* See Appendix D.

I was in the hope of finding some document or other, bearing on the Skipmyre and Kinharvey Patersons, 1650–1700, in the sheriff's records at Dumfries, or the steward's records at Kirkcudbright, or the burgh records at Dumfries. Mr Henry Gordon, sheriff-clerk of Dumfries, Mr George Hamilton, sheriff-clerk of Kirkcudbright, and Mr William Martin, town-clerk of Dumfries, kindly obliged me by turning over the several records in their hands applicable to the remote period referred to. Their searches were unavailing, no deeds or documents of the Patersons being discovered in any of these registers.

I referred also to the Duke of Queensberry's rental-book—the barony of Tinwald (Skipmyre included) having belonged for long to the Queensberry family—in the hope of finding John Paterson's name entered in it, 1650–1700. But the earliest entry of Skipmyre farm in the rental shewn me, was for crop 1760, when those Tinwald lands were stated to have been acquired by Charles Duke of Queensberry and Dover, from Charles Ariskine of Alva,* Esq., and the Honourable Alexander Dalyell of Glenae. The transfer from Glenae to the Duke of Queensberry, as I discovered elsewhere, was in or about 1748. The printed Register of Abbreviates of Special Retours, September 2,

---

* Charles Erskine of Alva, eldest son of Sir John Erskine, the second baronet,—a descendant of the Marr family, and of whom the noble house of Rosalyn has its ancestry,—born 1680, was a Lord of Session, as Lord Tinwald, and Lord Justice-Clerk, 1748. His son, James Erskine of Barjarg, as Lord Alva in the Court of Session, died the oldest judge in Britain in 1796.

1686, bore that John Dalyell, of Glenae, Bart., had been served heir-male of taillie of Robert Dalyell, · of Glenae, Bart., in the lands of Amisfield and many others; also in the lands of Trailflatt of Auchnane, with *Skipmyre*, Hunterhouse, with marshes of the same; also the forty-shilling land of Craigshield and Dalcrum, &c., &c., all united in the barony of Glenae. It would then be the Glenae rentals or tacks, could they be found, that would inform respecting the tenancy of Skipmyre at the period in question. Messrs J. & H. G. Gibson, W.S., Edinburgh, agents for his Grace the Duke of Buccleuch, obligingly allowed me access to the above mentioned Queensberry rental-book. But my efforts to get at the old rentals and tacks of the barony of Glenae, before Skipmyre was disjoined from it, have proved unsuccessful.

The register of births, marriages, and deaths, instituted by the Church of Scotland, in the earliest period of its history, and continued down to 1st January 1855, when superseded by the New General Registration Act of her present Majesty, 17 and 18 Victoria, chapter 80, had ofttimes been referred to in quest of William Paterson's birth and parentage. As we have already seen, the kirk-session kept minutes of their discipline proceedings from the commencement of Mr Robinson's ministry — the first Presbyterian minister in Tinwald and Trailflatt after the restoration of Presbytery. We cannot doubt that at the same time the kirk-session would have a register for parochial births, marriages, and deaths. In the early

volumes the marriages and deaths of John Paterson's
family would appear : for instance, the marriage and death
of Mrs Mounsey, the marriage of Bethia to Kinharvey,
and the deaths of the father and mother. What came of
those early registration volumes, or when they disappeared, is now unknown. Probably they were extant
when the Rev. Mr Lawrie wrote his Statistical Account
in 1785. All we know for certain is, that the existing
Tinwald and Trailflatt register commences so recently as
1762 ; *cetera desunt.*

In such circumstances the parochial registers afford no
information respecting Tinwald and Trailflatt births and
parentages, in the seventeenth century. I found the
registers for the adjoining parishes of Dumfries, Torthorwald, Kirkmichael, and Lochmaben, extant in good condition, and examined them, in case Skipmyre had married
his wife, Bethia Paterson, from one of them, but failed
in discovering any such entry. I wished to examine the
Newabbey parish register also, lest either husband or
wife, (the father and mother of the banker,) had been
of the Kinharvey Patersons. But the Newabbey
register had not been transmitted to Edinburgh. I was,
however, kindly obliged by the Rev. A. H. Charteris, now
in Park Church, Glasgow, late minister of Newabbey,
searching the registers there for me, and giving me some
extracts. I have myself since examined the registers at
Newabbey, but without finding anything to connect the
Skipmyre and Kinharvey Patersons previous to the mar-

riage of 1701. In this I was willingly aided by Mr John Paterson, schoolmaster, Newabbey, a namesake, but no connexion of the Patersons we are here seeking after.

In the New Register House, Mr Seton, the secretary, allowed me free access to the large collection therein of parochial registers of births, marriages, and deaths, down to 1819 inclusive, being those which were taken from the kirk-sessions of Scotland. They are being examined by Mr Patton, the chief clerk, leaf by leaf, with very great care, arranged according to counties, pasted where needful on interleaves, and bound up in hundreds of uniform-sized volumes. This work of what may be called parochial genealogical regeneration is far advanced. All facility is thereby afforded to persons in Edinburgh for getting at the vast fund of genealogical information with which the family history of many past generations has gorged those records under the superintending care of the Church of Scotland. Many of them date from the middle or latter end of the sixteenth century, and all will now be conserved for future generations in the archives of the New Register House. The parochial registers of births, marriages, and deaths, 1820-54, remain with the parish registrars—the statute, for what reason does not appear, not having ordered their transmission from the parishes to Edinburgh. On and after 1st January 1855, when the new system commenced, the statute ordered the registers of births, marriages, and deaths, to be kept in duplicate by the local registrars—one to be retained on the spot, always accessible in the locality, and the other to be transmitted annually to Edinburgh.

Of the children of John Paterson and Bethia Paterson, spouses, we should now endeavour to take account. These consisted, so far as known, of William, the banker, born 1658, and after him, Janet, (Mrs Mounsey or Muncie,) and Bethia or Elizabeth, (Mrs Paterson of Kinharvey.)   The tombstone II. bears that James Paterson, son of John, died 5th April 1694, followed by John and William Paterson.   The tombstone III. records John's death in February 1694; that John Paterson possibly was the banker's grandfather. At any rate, though of the same family, from his burying in that ground, along with several of the Mounceys, (stone III.,) he was necessarily a different person from John mentioned in the kirk-session minute of 1797, and who was party to the marriage-contract of 1701, and father of the banker.

A record obligingly communicated to me by Mr Francis Maxwell, of Breoch, Dumfries, mentions a Joseph Paterson, in Skipmyre—possibly some collateral relation of the banker. Thus : " April 20, 1736—Sold Joseph Paterson in Skipmyre, drover, 35 bullocks, at 21 lb. per each ; payt. him his luckpenny, and got ane bill for 50 lib. sterling, payable at the first of June 20 lib, and the oyr thirty at Lambas ; also got his bill for ten pounds sterling, payable at Lambas." *

* Memorandum book of John Macartney of Halketteaths.   The

William, as set forth very plainly in his will, married first Mrs Elizabeth Turner, widow of Thomas Bridge, minister of the gospel in Boston, New England, and next Mrs Hannah Kemp—her former husband's name and designation not mentioned. Admittedly on all hands he had no children by either; he died childless. Mrs Turner or Bridge had an only child, Elizabeth, by her first husband, whom the banker styles in his will, his "daughter-in-law,"—we would say "step-daughter." Mrs Kemp, the second wife, had four daughters and a son, styled in his will "daughters-in-law," and "son-in-law." To those step-daughters and to a step-son's widow he left legacies amounting to £4600; to his Scotch blood relations, the two sons and daughters of his sister Janet, Mrs Mounsey, he left legacies amounting to £1000; to his only sister, meaning his only sister then surviving, Elizabeth, Mrs Paterson, he left £800; to his executor, Paul Daranda, he left £1000;—any surplus there might be of his estate to be divided among the same parties in proportion to the sums bequeathed to them.

Of William Paterson, as already stated, there is not any entry in the Scottish registers of births, marriages, and

above transaction corresponds with one which is recorded as having occurred in the same market, (Dumfries,) in the same year:— "Cattle were very low. I remember being present at the Bridge-end of Dumfries in 1736, when Anthony M'Kie of Netherlaw sold five score of five-year-old Galloway cattle in good condition to an Englishman at £2, 12s. 6d. each." Letter of Mr John Maxwell of Munshes to Mr W. M. Herries of Spottes, dated February 1811. —*Murray's Lit. Hist. of Galloway.*

deaths. Had there been a birth register for Tinwald and Trailflatt in 1658, which in those troubled days in Dumfriesshire is exceedingly improbable, and had it been preserved to us for these two centuries bypast, we should have found William's birth therein—assuming, as may truly be done in consistency with the Statistical Account, that the parents were in Skipmyre when the birth took place. Paterson's two marriages must have occurred in England, at least furth of Scotland, and would not enter any Scottish register—hence no record of them in this country. Of the death, which Mr Bannister sets down, on the authority of the periodicals of the day, as having happened somewhere in Westminster or London, on 22d January 1719, he has not found any parochial record, though we doubt not further search in the burial registers of those cities may yet discover it. The nonregistration of the infant birth in Tinwald in 1658, when registrations were rare and compulsory registration wholly unknown, can easily be supposed and excused; the nonregistration of the death in the metropolis in 1719 of a man, world-wide in celebrity, is an omission of too grave a character to have happened. Of the resting-place of the deceased's remains nothing certain is known. No stone anywhere exists to direct

> " pale Scotia's way,
> To pour her sorrows o'er his honour'd dust."

The banker's will gives no direction to the executor respecting the place of interment. He there records him-

self as "of Westminster;" he certified his will at the
Ship Tavern without Temple Bar; he left the principal
part of all he had to step-children of his two wives; his
own native place is not named or alluded to in the will,
and his sisters and their children come last and least in
the list of legatees. Unless for his bequest to his sister
Bethia or Elizabeth, as spouse of Paterson younger of
Kinharvey in the stewartry of Kirkcudbright, no notion
could have been formed from the will that Paterson
had connexions of any kind in Scotland. But fortunately,
his mention of Mrs Paterson, and Mrs Paterson's own
genealogy in her marriage-contract, establish, as we have
already said, the parentage of her brother the banker
himself.

Though the parochial records and the other principal
registers of Scotland consulted by us, appear silent respecting the father and mother, John Paterson and
Bethia Paterson, down to 1697 and 1701, and appear
silent altogether respecting William Paterson their son,
it so happens that much information is contained in
them respecting the banker's sisters, Janet and Elizabeth.

1. Janet. That important document, the will, testifies
that she had four children : William—possibly named
after his uncle the banker—Elizabeth, Janet, and John
Mounsey. The family tree bears the father's name to
have been Thomas Mounsey, merchant, London; that he
came to reside at Skipmyre for recovery of his wife Janet

Paterson's health—so inferring that upon the marriage, the Mounseys had taken up house in London; that Mrs Mounsey died in 1698; that the husband married a second wife, Mary Steel, and died 6th August 1711, aged fifty-five. This harmonises with the inscriptions on the tombstones, and with the contract of marriage 1701, where "Thomas Muncie in Skipmyre," brother-in-law to Elizabeth, Mrs Paterson, was the first witness to the infeftment on her marriage-contract. The son, William Muncie or Mounsey, was also a witness and one of the legatees of the banker. The younger son, John Mounsey, had followed his uncle's steps to London, and got into employment there; at least Mr Bannister believes (and we agree with him) that John Mounsey is the same who subscribes "J. Mounsey" upon a copy bill of the directors of the Equivalent Debt, enclosed in a letter of Paterson (Westminster, 8th December 1718) to Earl Stanhope,—this "letter being the last trace hitherto found of William Paterson, who died in January following."—"Life," p. cxxvii.

From the marriage between Janet Paterson and Thomas Mounsey a numerous progeny flowed, and many descendants of theirs are to be found comfortably circumstanced in various localities and in various situations in life. Their leading branch held on by the farm of Skipmyre, in succession to John Paterson or Joseph Paterson, down till the recent date of 1844, when, after a duration of more than two centuries, the tenancy of that farm by the

Paterson family and their Mounsey descendants came to
an end. Mr Alexander Mounsey, the last Skipmyre pos-
sessor, then quitted the farm and settled in America.

The records of Tinwald parish, as we have already
seen, mention Thomas Mounsey as an acting kirk-session
elder in the end of the seventeenth century; and the
same record bears that his son William Mounsey was also
an acting elder in the early part of the eighteenth century. Again, from the Queensberry rental-book already
referred to, we learn that Alexander Mounsey, after
William, had a tack of Skipmyre farm for thirty-eight
years, from Whitsunday 1768, under condition that he
was to pay an additional rental of £38, to commence
from Whitsunday 1787. The rental adds, "Mounsey
(Alexander) is since dead, and the farm is possessed by
his son." At the Rev. Mr Lawrie's admission to the
parish in 1784, this Alexander Mounsey, grand-nephew of
the banker, farmed Skipmyre, and would be one of the
sources whence Mr Lawrie drew the information for
his statement in the Statistical Account, that the banker
had been born in Skipmyre. It is not our province
farther to trace the descendants of this most interesting
(Mounsey) branch of John Paterson's family.

In reference to Dr James Mounsey, already mentioned
as only son of Thomas Mounsey's second marriage with
Mary Steele, and also born in Skipmyre house, Mr Bannister has committed the mistake ("Life," p. xxxiii.) of
calling him "Paterson's nephew," whereas, being son of

Thomas Mounsey, not by Janet Paterson, but by Mary Steele, second wife, Dr Mounsey was no relation whatever to the banker. Possibly the Rev. Mr Lawrie had led Mr Bannister into this mistake; for Mr Lawrie, in his Statistical Account, erroneously styles Dr Mounsey as " grand-nephew" of the banker. It is interesting, however, to record, on the information of Mr Charles Stewart of Hill-side, a gentleman thoroughly versed in Dumfriesshire family history, that various Scotch physicians settled at St Petersburgh about the middle of the eighteenth century, or earlier—among them Dr Mounsey, who (as is well known) reached the top of the tree, and attained the distinguished position of physician to the Emperor and Empress of Russia. Dr Mounsey returned from Russia rather before 1770, and purchased the estate of Rammer-scales in Annandale, which he improved extensively, and where he built what was then considered a large and spacious mansion. He died soon after. The family tree bears his death to have happened in Edinburgh on 2d February 1773. My maternal grandfather, John Cunningham, was in Dr Mounsey's service at Rammerscales, when carrying on his improvements, and called a son after him Thomas Mounsey Cunningham.*

Mr Stewart also mentions, that after Dr Mounsey's return he advised Dr Rogerson, a connexion of his family, to follow his steps and settle in Russia. Dr Rogerson, then in his twenty-fifth year, acted on Dr Mounsey's

* See Appendix E.

advice, (1772,) and being a man of remarkable ability and intelligence, combined with dignified manners, he got immediately into high practice, and within three or four years became physician to the court. He remained forty years in Russia, and on his return acquired the estate of Dumcrieff in Annandale, an estate which passed to Lord Rollo on his marriage with Dr Rogerson's daughter and heiress. Mr Stewart adds, that the son of another Annandale farmer, a Halliday, with whom Dr Mounsey was intimate, also settled in St Petersburgh. Dr Halliday's great-grandson was lately Lieutenant-Governor in Bengal, under the Earl of Dalhousie, and is now Sir Frederick Halliday. These three medical men were all sons of neighbouring Annandale farmers. Mr Stewart has my best thanks for the information so kindly and readily afforded me.

2. Elizabeth, (Bethia.) This daughter, as already seen, married a Paterson of Kinharvey, in the stewartry of Kirkcudbright; and we gleaned a good deal of intelligence respecting her and her family from the Register of Land Rights, the Particular Register of Sasines kept at Dumfries, and from the Newabbey parish registers; also from titles of the lands of Kinharvey, through the obliging kindness of Mr Francis Maxwell of Breoch, (already mentioned,) factor for the Honourable Marmaduke Constable Maxwell of Terregles, now proprietor of Kinharvey. The lands of Kinharvey, otherwise Clocklowie, in the parish of Newabbey and stewartry of Kirkcudbright, were acquired

by John Paterson, (first of Kinharvey,) as is vouched by
instrument of resignation, dated 11th June 1618, in the
hands of the Privy Council, upon disposition by John Hay,
common clerk of Edinburgh, dated 19th December 1617.
This was confirmed by David Bishop of Edinburgh, by
charter in favour of John Paterson, dated 15th June 1637,
and he infeft thereon and his sasine registered in the
same Particular Register at Dumfries 10th August 1637.

John Paterson, (second,) son and heir of the above John,
was infeft in the same lands, and his sasine registered at
Dumfries 23d January 1672. In the following year he infeft Margaret Affleck his wife in an yearly annual rent of
£40, payable out of Kinharvey, and her sasine was registered at Dumfries 30th June 1673. It had been on this
precedent, that John, (third,) the eldest son of that marriage, settled a like annuity on Elizabeth Paterson in his
marriage-contract with her of 1701. That same contract
performed the twofold service of conveying Kinharvey
from John (second) to his son John, (third,) reserving a
liferent to the father and Margaret Affleck his wife, and
of securing John's (third) wife in her liferent annuity.
See the two sasines, Appendix. Among the witnesses to
the two sasines were Thomas Muncie, (Mounsey,) in Skipmyre, and William Muncie, (Mounsey,) his son, the brother-in-law and nephew of the banker. Titles to land in
Scotland were completed, from 1617, by five or more
persons travelling to and standing on the ground of the
lands—the notary, procurator, baillie, and witnesses, a

practice continued till the abolition of such sasines, by recent statutes simplifying Scotch conveyancing. Those selected to assist the notary on the occasion were frequently, as in the above instance, relatives or friends of the parties giving or receiving the infeftment.

John (third) fortified his title to Kinharvey by serving himself heir in special to his father,—the service retoured to Chancery 18th May 1725; a precept following thereon dated 10th August 1725; and finally sasine in his favour, dated 2d September, and registered in the Particular Register at Dumfries 3d September 1725. He afterwards executed a trust-disposition of Kinharvey in favour of William Gracie of Wester Glen, narrating that John Paterson, (fourth,) his only son and heir, was abroad, and his return uncertain, and conveying Kinharvey for his behoof, provided he returned within nine years, and for other purposes; this trust-disposition bears date 27th April 1739. Kinharvey did not long survive the execution of the above trust-deed; for the records of the Commissary of Dumfries bear that he died in June 1739, and that an inventory of his personal estate was given up by his widow, Elizabeth (Bethia) Paterson, the banker's sister, still surviving. The inventory was very full and particular; one entry in it, for instance, being—"Item, Some old body clothes of the defunct's, and a pair old boots, worth 14s." "Total, £xc. 8s. 3d." (supposed Scots.) In this judicial act, William Muncie in Skipmyre, nephew of Mrs Paterson and the banker, stands as cautioner for

D

the widow's due administration of the Kinharvey exe-
cutry.*

William Gracie, the trustee, with consent of John Paterson, (fourth,) returned, sold and disponed Kinharvey

* The Commissary records we examined in the Register House,
Edinburgh, from the beginning of the seventeenth century till the
end of the eighteenth, but without finding any Skipmyre inventory
therein, or other document than the Kinharvey one of 1740 above
mentioned. This was an easy part of our task, there being a
legibly-written nominal index to the whole inventories in the
record recently prepared, evidently the work of much care and
labour. Easy and certain reference is thereby afforded to each
inventory in these records. Under the attractive name, "Robert
Burns," we found the whole personalty given up by Mrs Jean
Armour, his widow, as amounting to only fifteen pounds :—"1796,
Oct. 6. Robert Burns, officer of excise in Dumfries, died July
1796. Inventory given up by Jean Armour, his relict—no will.
1st, Sum of £5 contained in promissory-note, Sir Wm. Forbes &
Co., (bankers, Edinburgh,) to George Shearer, payable on demand,
indorsed payable to defunct. 2d, £10 in draft, dated 15th July
1796, by Robert Christie, on British Linen Co., Edinburgh, in
favour of James Burness, indorsed by him to defunct. *Summa* of
inventory, fifteen pounds. William Wallace, writer, Dumfries,
cautioner." This inventory should also have included the library
and household furniture, and any other moveable estate of the poet.
Dr Robert Chambers's Life of Burns, vol. iv., p. 223, informs us
that the poet owed only a few pounds at his death, while there belonged to him a sum of £180, due to him by his brother, books to
the value of £90, and his household furniture. But the purpose
of the inventory, plainly and simply, was to warrant the uplifting
by the widow of the two bank orders which had come to her husband—too late, however, to be of any use to him. The two
sums above mentioned were remittances made to the poet on his
death-bed, in compliance with urgent requests from him—the former by George Thomson of Edinburgh, the latter by James Burness of Montrose, (his relative,) as particularly mentioned by

to John Pain in Conguth, by disposition dated 23d June
1748—and so this romantic little estate (as it has been
called) was passed away from the Patersons, after being
in their hands fully one hundred and thirty years. Pain

Burns's biographers. The poet died nearly seven years before I was
born, but I recollect Mrs Burns, the widow, and Mr Wallace, the
cautioner, quite well. When a boy at Dumfries School, 19th June
1815, the day after Wellington's crowning victory at Waterloo, I
witnessed Burns's second interment—the removal of his body from
its first resting-place near the centre of Dumfries churchyard, to
the public mausoleum then erected in honour of his memory.
His widow had an annuity of £60 from the sale of Currie's edition
of Burns, or other generous sources, which was paid her monthly
in Mr Thomson's office, where I was apprenticed. Not coming,
one first of the month, or sending, the cashier, Mr Robert M'Lellan,
lately deceased, took me along with him to Mrs Burns's house—
the house where the poet died—when the widow thanked us kindly
for calling with the money, and gave us wine and cake. It is no
small matter to have received such from the hand of "bonnie
Jean." That would be in 1819 or 1820. Mrs Burns lived till 1834,
having survived her husband thirty-eight years. The same physician, Dr William Maxwell of Dumfries, who ministered most
kindly to the poet on his death-bed, was successful in carrying me
through a severe fever which afflicted me in boyhood. I was present at the great Burns festival on the banks of the Doon, on 6th
August 1844, where the Earl of Eglintoun presided, assisted by
Professor Wilson, the late Lord Justice General (Boyle,) Sir Archi-
bald Alison, Bart., and other Scotsmen of mark, and where my
father introduced me to Burns's three sons, Lieut.-Col. Burns,
Major Burns, and Mr Robert Burns. I was also present at the
Edinburgh centenary meeting on 25th January 1859, in honour of
Burns, where Lord Ardmillan presided, and where I happened to
sit next that aged man, Mr Walter Glover, from Craigmillar, near
Edinburgh, (since deceased,) then one hundred and one years of
age, who told me what he had seen of Burns at Dumfries, and of
transactions he had been engaged in three or four generations back.

again sold to Mr Wilson,—Wilson to Mr Gordon,—Gordon to Mr Riddell, (whom I remember as proprietor and residenter at Kinharvey,) and Riddell to the Honourable Marmaduke Constable Maxwell of Terregles, now the proprietor. The same Maxwell family owned the lands in 1611, (at least in superiority,) and in the mutability of human affairs, have thus regained them after a lapse of more than two centuries. The Abbreviate printed register of special retours of land bears:—"1611. Joannes (Maxwell) Dominus Herries, *hæres* Gulielmi Domini Herries, *patris*, in 40 solidatis terrarum de Kinhervie et Clockloy antiqui extentus in parochia de New Abbey, E 105."

Of the Kinharvey heirs female, I find several mentioned in the records. John Paterson, (second,) had a daughter Janet,—(his eldest daughter,)—married to John Morrison, of Culloch, in Urr. She was infeft in his lands of Culloch, in security of the jointure, provided in the marriage-contract between them; her sasine stands in the Particular Register at Dumfries, of date 11th October 1699. The same John Paterson (married to Margaret Affleck) is recorded in the baptisms for Newabbey parish as having further had a daughter, Elizabeth, baptized June 7, 1691; a son, Adam, June 1, 1691, (supposed twins;) and a son, Thomas, May 8, 1693.

John (third) and Bethia or Elizabeth Paterson, appear from the same register to have had these children baptized—January 11, 1716, a son, William, probably named after his uncle, the banker; June 23, 1722, a daughter,

Nicholas; and June 24, 1724, a son Ebenezer. Those sons, William and Ebenezer, had died previous to 1739—at least in the father's trust-deed to Gracie in that year, he speaks of John (fourth) as his only son and heir. This John (fourth) does not appear in the baptismal register. Nicholas, the daughter, married John Carson, merchant in Dumfries, and a discharge by these spouses in favour of Gracie, the trustee, of a provision by her father in Mrs Carson's favour, is registered in the Particular Register of Sasines at Dumfries January 8, 1755. Her brother John (fourth) returned, was then alive and a party to the discharge. She is therein named "Nicholas Paterson, youngest lawful daughter of the deceased John Paterson of Kinharvey." Nicholas had a son James Carson; and his eldest son, Mr William Carson, stocking maker, 77 Queensberry Square, Dumfries, represents this branch —Mr Carson being great-grandson of the banker's sister, Elizabeth or Bethia Paterson of Kinharvey.

We found the burying-place of the Kinharvey Patersons within the walls of Sweetheart Abbey, marked by a stone lying on the floor inscribed with what was once a lengthened Latin epitaph, but now nearly defaced. All we could make out, with the assistance of Mr John Paterson, schoolmaster, was that the "Paterson" there interred was "*probus vir* "—" *obijt* 1719 "—" æt. 73." He would be the father-in-law of Bethia Paterson, married 1701. It would be well were the above stone raised up and set on supports, after the manner of the kindred ones at Trailflatt, and the inscription retouched by the renovating chisel of some kind "old mortality."

In the register of marriages for the parish of Dumfries, I found the following entry applicable to another daughter of Kinharvey :—"26th May 1728. — William Endsly, (Ainslie?) squareman in this burgh, and Mary Paterson, daughter to John Paterson of Kinharvey, in the parish of Newabbey, after proclamation were lawfully married." As a daughter of John and Bethia Paterson, Mary was a niece of the banker. We did not turn to the Dumfries birth-registers in quest of descendants from this marriage, nor indeed further pursue the Kinharvey branch of the family—though such could be done with ease and probable certainty in the middle and end of the eighteenth century, as compared with genealogical researches at earlier periods in defective and difficult records.

Mr Bannister, as already said, knew not the names of Paterson's father and mother, or anything authentic concerning them. He has not hesitated, however, to speak almost as if they, and all their ancestors too, had been his familiar acquaintances. We find him saying—(Writings, vol. i. p. xix.) :—" His father's family, the Patersons, were eminent of old, and in his time they had representatives among the high modern Episcopalians and adherents of the house of Stuart. They had descended from an ancient Scandinavian stock, originally planted in Northumberland, and had not been without distinction on both sides the Border."

Whencever the original Paterson of Skipmyre had descended—whether from Northumberland, or Scandinavia, or elsewhere, clear enough is it that the surname "Paterson" came not from foreign parts, but originated in England or Scotland, by simply adding "son" to the earlier name of Peter or Patrick. Thus going back to one of our earliest records—the Inventory of the Records of Scotland between 1309 and 1413, recovered in the end of last century by Mr William Robertson, one of the Deputies of the Lord Clerk Register for keeping the records of Scotland,*—we find that King Robert Second granted a charter to William, son of William of the Brewland of Methven, on a resignation by "Roger son of Patrick." We find also another charter by the same monarch, confirming a grant by James Douglas of Dalkeith, to David son of Peter. These Mr Robertson indices as "PATERSON, (Peterson, Patrickson.)" We may thus hold that the Peters and Patricks of ancient days

* The title of Mr Robertson's valuable volume is :—" An Index, (drawn up about the year 1629,) of many records of charters granted by the different sovereigns of Scotland, between the years 1309 and 1413, most of which records have been long missing, with an introduction giving a state founded on authentic documents still preserved of the ancient records of Scotland, which were in that kingdom in the year 1292. To which are subjoined indices of the persons and places mentioned in those charters, alphabetically arranged. Published at the desire of The Right Honourable Lord Frederick Campbell, Lord Clerk Register of Scotland, with a view to lead to the discovery of those records which are missing. By William Robertson, Esq. Edinburgh : Murray and Cochrane, 1798."

originated, in their descendants, so many Petersons, Patricksons, and Patersons, in the same way as the Adams, and Bryces, and Cars, founded the Adamsons, Brysons, and Carsons, whom we now have. Any attempt to trace such from other countries would be vain.

Mr Bannister mentions John Paterson, the last Archbishop of Glasgow, as a contemporary of the banker. Not the slightest relationship was there between them. Of the Archbishop we are told by Mr Alexander Peterkin, in his Abridgment of the Acts of the General Assembly of the Church of Scotland, (Edinburgh 1831,) as follows:— "John Paterson, son of John Paterson, Bishop of Ross, was first a minister at Ellon in Aberdeenshire, afterwards minister of the Tron Church and Dean of Edinburgh, and was appointed Bishop of Galloway 23th October 1674, in which see he continued till 29th March 1679, when he was translated to that of Edinburgh, where he continued till 1687. He was promoted to the Archiepiscopal see of Glasgow, of which he was deprived at the revolution in 1688. He died at Edinburgh, 8th December 1706, in the seventy-sixth year of his age."

In the outset of the Life, (p. 2,) Mr Bannister introduces the celebrated John Law of Lauriston as a "relative" of Paterson, though no relationship, in the ordinary sense, appears to have existed between them. Writing playfully in the "Scot Abroad," Mr Hill Barton placed Law and Paterson together, but not as relatives. He said, (p. 278,) "On the Plutarchian system of comparison, John Law and William Paterson should pair off together—the one as having ruined France with the Mississippi scheme, the other as having ruined Scotland with the Darien scheme. They had other parallel conditions in life, in that they were competitors for laying schemes before their own countrymen. Law had proposed certain projects to the parliament of Scotland, which being in a cautious humour they declined to adopt, and he then carried his genius abroad. Paterson's schemes were all directed to the aggrandisement of his own country, and therefore he does not appear at first sight within the category of those Scotsmen whose genius and achievements have been exhibited among foreigners. But Paterson, during a large part of his life, was busy abroad. His practical information on foreign countries guided the Darien Company and the Scottish parliament in all their operations."

Mistakenly, Mr Bannister says the banker had a *brother*, "who gave considerable funds to the town of Dumfries in aid of the old schools, and expressly extended the subjects of study to navigation."* The generous individual here referred to by Mr Bannister was John Paterson, merchant and bailie in Dumfries, but not a Skipmyre man, nor a Dumfriesshire man, nor a relative,— certainly not a brother of the banker. The statistical account (1791) which Mr Bannister accepts as authority for William Paterson's birthplace in Tinwald tells us that

* Life, p. 36.

Bailie Paterson was a native of the (Newabbey) parish; he also erected the bridge at the entry to the village from Dumfries, as is commemorated by the following inscription: "Erected by Bailie John Paterson, late of Dumfries, 1715."

Respecting Bailie Paterson we are further informed by the New Statistical Account 1840, per the Rev. James Hamilton, many years minister of the parish, that a farm now yielding so much as £190 sterling of yearly rent, was purchased in 1756 for behoof of the poor of Newabbey, chiefly with money (£156) left by Bailie Paterson and its accumulations. The purchase money was £220. In the Newabbey kirk-session records we were shewn a volume containing a clear account of Bailie Paterson's bequest to the minister and elders for behoof of the poor of that his native parish—commencing with a copy assignation by him, dated 25th June 1714, where he designed himself "one of the present Bailies of Dumfries." The land investment by the kirk-session of Bailie Paterson's money had been singularly successful and productive, the poors funds drawing now the above handsome rental of £190 sterling therefrom, a striking instance of the increase in the value of land in Galloway.

In the Particular Register of Sasines kept at Dumfries, of date 5th April 1722, I found a full record of Bailie Paterson's generous benefactions to the Dumfries schools contained in two sasines upon dispositions (mortifications) by him in favour of the provost, ministers, magis-

trates, and councillors of the burgh of Dumfries. The
monies settled by him on these trustees consisted of
15,000 merks, equal, at 1s. 1¼d. per merk, to £833, 6s. 8d.
sterling, a large sum in those days. They were secured
partly over the twenty-four merkland of Prestown, with
the merse and fell of Criffel, in the parish of Kirkbean,
barony of Prestown and stewartry of Kirkcudbright;
the eight merkland of Kirkbean and the eight merkland
of Nimbellie and Fallowend, lying in the said parish;
and partly over the seven merkland half merkland of
Meikle Culloch, lying in the parish of Urr and stewartry
foresaid.

Bailie Paterson's educational objects were twofold.
By one deed he settled 7000 merks, equal to £388, 17s.
9¼d. sterling, on the above Dumfries trustees, and their
successors in office, or major part of them, "for the use,
behoof, alimenting, and maintaining ane well qualified
schoolmaster, and teaching and instructing of the youth
and children of burgesses who shall be indwellers and
burden-bearers, and of eight children of the poorer sort
of merchant burgesses and burden-bearers in the said
burgh, in the arts of writing, arithmetic, book-keeping,
and navigation." By his other deed he settled 8000
merks—equal to £444, 8s. 10⅔d. sterling—on Janet
Gracie his wife, who survived him, in liferent, and of the
foresaid trustees, "for the use, behoof, alimenting, and
maintaining ane well qualified schoolmaster within the
said burgh of Dumfries for teaching and instructing of

youth and children in ane free school perpetually to the
end of the world, without any fee or reward, in the Latin
rudiments and grammar, rhetoric and classic authors, and
Greek New Testament." The sasines from which we are
making these quotations were both registered at Dumfries
on the date above mentioned, (5th April 1722,) shortly
previous to which the worthy and thoughtful donor had
died.

Of Bailie Paterson's educational foundations, I am
entitled to speak with all respect, having myself under the
second of them enjoyed (or endured) a five or six years'
curriculum in the classical department of the Dumfries
Academy, 1811-1816, without fee or reward, further than
the customary, at least then customary, Candlemas
gratuity, from the pupils to Dr George Monro the rector.
I recollect of an objection being started by the Dumfries
authorities to boys resident on the Galloway side of the
Nith (as happened with me) getting free classical education; but the objection was not pressed nor could be, my
father being a burgess of the town. It would have been
unfortunate indeed, had a Galloway man excluded a
Galloway boy from benefiting by his educational endowment. It is quite a satisfaction to me that through
Mr Bannister's mistaking that generous Gallovidian
Bailie John Paterson for a Dumfriesshire man, for a
brother of the banker, I have been led to make this
brief mention of his birthplace and of his good deeds;—
Galloway, we may believe, being as anxious to hold by

her son John Paterson, as Dumfriesshire is to hold by the more distinguished William Paterson for her son.

The town-clerk of Dumfries, Mr William Martin, obliged me by examining the old records of Dumfries, but reported nothing found in them respecting Bailie Paterson, save the two above-mentioned sasines of 1722, of which I had previously become possessed in the Particular Register. The annual printed account of the town, 1863, bears : — " Debts—Irredeemable mortifications, £1370 ; " and on the other side, " Salaries to Teachers, £71, 4s. 10d.," but no mention of a founder's name. In the absence of any clear statement, we are left to conjecture that £833, 6s. 8d. of the above "irredeemable mortifications," (as they are called,) belong to Bailie Paterson's funds, and that a corresponding part of the salaries has arisen from the interest. There being, however, two separate trusts, for separate purposes, apart altogether from the ordinary funds and management of the town, there ought to be (and may be) separate accounts, shewing the trust income annually received and how applied. Such are desirable for the information of those intended to be benefited, as well as to keep the founder's name in deserved remembrance, and prevent misconception respecting him, like that into which Mr Bannister has accidently fallen.

A collection of " Epitaphs and monumental inscriptions, chiefly in Scotland," (Glasgow, 1834,) contains the following under the head " Dumfries : " — " Here lieth the body of John Paterson, son to John Paterson, merchant in Dumfries, who died the 10th of November 1711 ; aged 16 years and eight months :—

> When parents, friends, and neighbours hoped to see,
> This early bud of learning, piety,
> And temper good, produce some fruit,
> Behold, Death plucks the plant up by the root."

My friend, Mr John Jackson of Amisfield, Dumfries, informs me that the stone with the above inscription still stands in the old churchyard, Dumfries; also that an adjoining stone records the death of Bailie Paterson, the father, in these terms :—"Here lies John Paterson, merchant, late bailie of Dumfries, who died 17th January 1722, aged 65 years." With all truth there might have been added :—"Bailie Paterson was a large benefactor to the public, having left considerable sums for the endowment of Dumfries schools, and built a bridge at Newabbey, and provided for the poor of Newabbey, his native parish." These two stones, in the old churchyard at Dumfries, are in the keeping of Mr William Carson of Dumfries, already mentioned as a descendant of Mrs Bethia Paterson of Kinharvey. No trace has anywhere appeared to me of a relationship betwixt Bailie Paterson and the Skipmyre and Kinharvey families. Indeed, these stones in Dumfries churchyard, first to Bailie Paterson's son, and then to Bailie Paterson himself, go to mark him as of different blood. Had he been of the same, we may implicitly believe that, in the predilection which there is in Scotland for adhering to family burying-grounds, the remains of both father and son would have been carried to Trailflatt or Newabbey, where lie the Skipmyres and Kinharveys. The fact of Bailie Paterson devoting his means to the public purposes above mentioned—subject only to a provision to his widow—indicates that he had not any immediate surviving relatives.*

Speaking on the authority of the deceased Mr Elliot Warburton, Mr Bannister says, ("Life," p. 39,) that the banker had to leave Dumfriesshire in his youth (1678?) owing to a charge against him of being "a confederate with the outlawed Presbyterians." Of this there does not seem to be any evidence. Had Paterson's father or his youthful son been involved in such a serious affair, surely

* In ancient times the building a public bridge by an individual was reckoned an act of piety. Thus in the same district, Devorgilla, daughter of Allan, first Lord of Galloway, and wife of John Comyn of Castle Barnard, a lady of distinguished piety and munificence, erected—1. New Abbey or Sweetheart Abbey, in this same parish of Newabbey, about seven miles from Dumfries, where, upon her death in 1289, at the age of eighty, she was buried, the embalmed heart of her husband, who had died twenty-nine years before, being buried with her. The ruin of this once magnificent ecclesiastical edifice attracts many admiring visitors. 2. She erected the Greyfriars Monastery in Dumfries, where Comyn was killed by Bruce and Kirkpatrick on 10th February 1305. The site of the monastery is well known, but of the buildings not a vestige is to be seen. 3. She erected the bridge—now truly the old bridge of Dumfries—that was in the reign of Alexander III. It consisted of thirteen arches, (now sadly curtailed,) and was described by Pemberton, in his journey through Scotland, 1723, as "a fair stone bridge of thirteen large arches, the finest I saw in Britain next to London and Rochester." Being the only access then existing

some reliable record of the fact would have been preserved.   Indeed, the long continuance of the Patersons
in the tenancy of Skipmyre attests, in the strongest
manner, that the family were both peaceable and indus-
trious, and not given to intermeddling of any kind.

The sixty-one short years of this distinguished man's
life formed an eventful epoch in British history.   They
witnessed the death of Cromwell; the brief protectorate
of Richard his son; the joyful restoration of King
Charles II.; the erection of turnpikes in England;
the ravages of the plague, and the great fire in London;
the twenty-nine years' endurance of Episcopacy in Scotland; the risings, and struggles, and persecutions of the
Covenanters; the murder of Archbishop Sharpe; the

betwixt the stewartry and Dumfries, Bailie Paterson would use
Devorgilla's Bridge in travelling betwixt Dumfries and his native
parish of Newabbey; and the circumstance of its being a contribu-
tion to the public from a private lady, may have led him to think
of a lesser, but similar work—the building of his Newabbey bridge.
There was a coincidence between the Lady Devorgilla and Bailie
Paterson, in each having devoted funds to three philanthropic
objects; the former to the building of an abbey, a monastery, and
a bridge; the latter to the endowing schools, providing for the
parochial poor, and building a bridge.   Though small in comparison, the bailie's foundations have outstood those of the lady; the
school endowment is still effectual, the provision for the poor is
not only preserved but vastly increased, and the Newabbey Bridge
(or a second edition of it) is still extant.   On the other hand,
Sweetheart Abbey is now no more than a splendid ruin; the
monastery has disappeared, and the Dumfries old bridge is on its
original and last legs—fairly worn out in nearly six hundred years'
service, and outrivalled by the handsome new bridge, built almost
alongside, in 1795.

penny post instituted in London; the death of Charles;
King James II.'s accession to the throne; the Duke of
Monmouth's rebellion; the abdication of the king; the
revolution which placed William and Mary on the throne;
the Irish rebellion; the Bank of England established,
and, next year, the Bank of Scotland; the massacre of
Glencoe; the projection and failure of the Scottish Darien
expedition; the deaths of William and Mary; the accession and reign of Queen Anne; the Union of England
and Scotland; the South Sea scheme; the death of Anne,
and the accession of King George I.; the rebellion of
1715; the battle of Sheriffmuir; and the Act of the British
Parliament, ordering £18,241, 10s. 10¾d. of compensation
money (a vast sum in those days) to Paterson, in respect
of his claims on the nation.

Paterson's important services and heavy outlays connected with the Darien expedition, are set forth in reports
by committees of the House of Commons, 1713 and 1715,
on which the Compensation Act in his favour proceeded.
The reports particularly bear that Paterson, in devoting
himself to the public service, had relinquished his business as a merchant in London,—a fact inconsistent
with the story that he occupied himself as a bucanier ·
abroad. Copies of these interesting state-papers are
in the hands of Dr David Laing of Edinburgh. The
statute was the first of George I., cap. ix., passed 1715,
and intituled, "An Act for relieving William Paterson,

E

Esq., out of the Equivalent Money, for what is due to him." *

It was from the fund provided or secured to him by this Act of 1715, that Paterson, as may be supposed, was enabled to leave the several legacies specified in his will

* The printed bill on which the Act proceeded is in these terms: — " Whereas by the fifteenth article of the Treaty of Union, it is agreed, That next after the necessary allowance for any losses which private persons may sustain by reducing the coyn of Scotland to the standard and value of the coyn of England, the capital stock or fund of the African and Indian Company of Scotland advanced, together with the interest for the said capital stock after the rate of five per cent. per annum, from the respective times of the payment thereof, shall be paid ; upon payment of which capital stock and interest, it is agreed the said company be dissolved and cease. And whereas, soon after passing the Treaty of Union by the Parliaments of both kingdoms, the Parliament of Scotland, by an act intituled, ' Act concerning the payment of the sums out of the Equivalent to the African Company,' did limit and restrict the payment of such interest of five per cent. per annum, to the 1st day of May 1707 then next following, and the whole sums of principal and interest, to be paid to the creditors and proprietors of the joint-stock of the said company, to the gross sum of £232,884, 5s. 0¾d. only ; appointing the directors of the said company, or any five of them, with their secretary, to state the account of such debts and stock advanced, but so as in the whole not to exceed the said gross sum of £232,884, 5s. 0¾d., on or before the said 1st day of May, on pain of letters of horning ; in which proceedings the claim and demand of William Paterson, Esq., upon the said company was omitted : And whereas, by an Act made in the first Parliament of Great Britain, intituled ' An Act for the further directing the payment of the Equivalent Money,' it is particularly declared and enacted, That no omission or neglect of the directors of the said company, or of others concerned, in stating, adjusting, or certifying the claims or demands upon the equivalent, shall prejudice the right, interest,

of 1718. The executor, Paul Daranda, stands high in the estimation of Mr Bannister—the two volumes of Writings being dedicated to his memory in very flattering terms. But in that opinion the Scotch relations would not concur—at least the present survivors are under the distinct

claim, or demand of the said William Paterson, in and upon the said company; but that the several sums due to him by the said company shall be certified, and thereupon fully satisfied and paid in the terms of the Treaty of Union, as the same shall be proved before the judges of the Court of Exchequer in Scotland : And whereas, by the proofs made before the said judges, pursuant to the above-recited special direction, it appears that the said William Paterson hath not received the considerations stipulated in and by his first contracts and agreements with the said company, nor had satisfaction for his further and other services, expenses, and losses for and on their account: May it therefore please your Majesty, that it may be enacted, and be it enacted, by the King's Most Excellent Majesty, by and with the advice and consent of the Lords Spiritual and Temporal, and Commons in this present Parliament assembled, and by authority of the same, that it shall and may be lawful for the Commissioners of the Equivalent, and they are hereby required and directed forthwith, to issue and pay to the said William Paterson, his executors, administrators, or assigns, the sum of £18,241, 10s. 10½d., in like debentures with those appointed to be issued by the aforesaid Act for the further directing the payment of the equivalent money. The principal money upon which debentures shall be payable in course, after payment of those issued, or which ought to have been issued, for the debts provided for by the said several Acts concerning the same; but the interest upon the said debentures, at the rate of five per cent. per annum, shall, from the 25th day of March 1713, be in the meantime payable in the same manner as upon the other debentures. And for the more easy and convenient assignment and transference thereof, such debentures are hereby particularly directed to be issued and made forth in sums of not more than five hundred pounds, nor in sums of less than one hundred pounds each."

impression that the legacies never were paid, and probably for this reason that the executor had not been able to
recover from the Treasury the full compensation money
ordered by the Act of Parliament to be paid to Paterson
or his heirs. At sundry times the Scotch relations made
searching investigations, but entirely without effect. Mr
Stewart of Hillside, a gentleman already named, has
obliged us with the perusal of notes of a "case" drawn
up for them in 1853, with a view to further inquiry.
That document leaves little doubt that the compensation
money, so justly due to Paterson, had not been realised
—certainly that the Scotch relatives never received the
legacies designed for them.

The handsome legacies in the will to the Mounseys,
and Mrs Paterson, Kinharvey, (paid or unpaid,) would all
the more keep their connexion with Paterson in continual
remembrance,—indeed, it was not in human nature that
they would fail constantly and proudly to recollect their
illustrious relative, and the high position to which his
genius had carried him.

The Scotch relations—particularly the Mounseys, descended of the banker's sister Janet,—occupied themselves
for years in endeavouring to trace the funds whence
the legacies should have been paid, but in vain. It was
in the prosecution of this that the family genealogical
tree, already mentioned, was prepared—shewing clearly
enough the increasing, and multiplying, and replenishing
which flowed from Janet's marriage with Thomas Moun-

sey. Paterson, we may assume, would get acquainted with Mounsey in London, where he was a merchant, and through that introduction the marriage would come about. The tree bears that Mounsey came to Skipmyre, with his wife in poor health, where she died in 1698; that he settled there; and entered into his second marriage with Mary Steel, of which Dr Mounsey was the fruit.

In this genealogical inquiry my researches were not among papers stored in great collections, such as the British Museum, the state-papers at the Tower or the Advocates' Library, where the writings of eminent men may be found. Hence I do not here present anything new from these sources; probably the industry of Mr Bannister in London has not left any material thing there unexplored. Of all the papers in Mr Bannister's volumes, one of the most interesting is Paterson's "Report of matters relating to the colony of Caledonia, made to the Right Honourable the Court of Directors of the Indian and African Company of Scotland," dated December 19, 1699. (Writings, vol. i., pp. lvii., lxxxviii.) That document recounts the chief incidents of the Darien expedition, from his sailing with it in July 1698, till its disastrous conclusion, and his return to Britain in December 1699. The report bears painful record of the author's sufferings from fever, but still more from trouble of mind, attendant on the crosses, and vexations, and heartbreaking miscarriage of the scheme on which he had set his heart. While penning these lines, the Bank of Scotland

is presenting to the Scottish Society of Antiquaries the
lock and keys of the Darien Company's treasure-chest,
perhaps the only actual relics now remaining of the expedition. (See Appendix F.) In modern times, specie supplies are no longer necessary accompaniments of those
proceeding on foreign undertakings,—for, before them,
nearly in every part of the globe, there are banking-
houses with cash ready to answer drafts,—correspon-
dents, probably, of those very banks founded in 1694
and 1695 by the wisdom of William Paterson.*

In the Commissary records of Dumfries and Kirkcudbright, I found an inventory of the estate of a namesake of
William Paterson, viz.,—"1687, July 29.—William Paterson, merchant in England, given up by William Paterson
in Howthat, Ruthwell," and where "Charles Paterson in

---

* The want of banks over Scotland at the period referred to is
aptly illustrated by the following minute, which we found in the
kirk-session record of Paterson's natal parish :—"At Tinwald,
March 28, 1700.—The minister reports that he received that 200
merks from Edward Walls, according to appointment, (being a
legacy from Andrew Walls, merchant, Glasgow,) and he gave him
a receipt y'of. The session, not knowing of a convenient hand to
lodge it in, they desired the minister to keep it in his hand till
such time as they got a secure hand to lodge it in ; that he pay the
annual rent therefor; which the minister condescended unto." The
Bank of Scotland, following the Bank of England, had been established a few years previously; but there were not then penny
posts, penny newspapers, railway trains, and electric telegraphs to
spread intelligence—not even stage coaches. Transit across the
country at that time would be uncertain, difficult, and tedious
enough.

Hayburns " is mentioned as a debtor. But no relation-ship appears to have existed between these Patersons and the banker. I did not find in the Commissary records, from 1639 downwards, any will or inventory applicable to Paterson in Skipmyre or the Mounseys.

Dumfriesshire and Galloway men, like the banker and the above William Paterson, merchant traveller in Eng-land, frequently crossed the Border in mercantile pursuits. Thus the same Commissary records bear :—" 1685, Octo-ber 12. John Pagane, merchant traveller, lately in England, now in Kirkbean, (Galloway,) brother-german to David Pagane in Byris"—his settlement, dated 4th June 1685, and inventory recorded. The name Pagan appears in the county and parochial registers of Dumfriesshire and Gal-loway for more than two centuries back. It originated near the close of the tenth century with a French crusader, who acquired it by his successes against the pagans or infidels. (See Appendix G.)

The name "Paterson" occurs pretty frequently in all the old Dumfries and Galloway registers. That for the parish of Dumfries contains entries of several children baptized to John Paterson in Kelwood, being the south-most farm in Dumfries parish. The first of these is—" 1611, April 21.—Baptized John, son to John Paterson in Kelwood—witnesses, Adam Patersone and Clement M'Burnie in Dumfries." This infant might have grown into John, father of the banker, born 1658, but I see no reason to believe that such was the fact, or that there was any relationship. Curiously enough, "John" was a prevailing name among the Patersons. The same parish register also bears:—"1690, January 23.—Baptized Robert, son to James Paterson in Tinwald—witness, John Paterson, merchant." This James in Tinwald could scarcely be the centenarian, born 1621. He might be a residenter in the *village* of Tinwald, and not at all connected with the Skipmyre family. The baptism in Dumfries may have been owing to a vacancy in the incumbency of Tinwald parish, or temporary absence of the clergyman. The witness, "John Paterson, merchant," would likely be Bailie Paterson, of whom we have already spoken. As often happened in the old registers, no mothers' names are given in those instances to assist in tracing the genealogy. I should add that nothing has come under my observation tending to show that the progenitors of William Paterson had had a settlement anywhere else than at the farm of Skipmyre in Tinwald.

Assuming that the evidence here gathered together and laid before the public has established in the clearest and fullest manner the birthplace and parentage of this remarkable man,—that his parents were John Paterson and Bethia Paterson, and his birthplace Skipmyre, in the old parish of Trailflatt, now Tinwald, Dumfriesshire, —we would venture a suggestion, that the fact should not be allowed to rest on transient tradition, or on scattered written or printed records, but that it should be forthwith attested by some fitting public monumental memorial to Paterson. The vicinity of Skipmyre farm-house, or the adjoining ridge betwixt Nithsdale and Annandale—Tinwald top,* about 700 feet high—would be a thing of beauty, an object of attraction, not merely to the "queen of the south," Dumfries, but to all within the magnificent amphitheatre amid which Tinwald proudly lifts its head. The lofty Queensberry and Hartfell would range on the north; Burnswark on the east; Criffel, and the silver Solway, and the Cumberland mountains on the south; and the hills of Galloway on the west. The monument would look down on the fertile plains of Nithsdale and Annandale, and find thousands of admiring spectators in the teeming trains of the Caledonian, the Glasgow and South-Western, the Dumfries and Lockerbie, and the Dumfries and Portpatrick Railway Companies. It would remind all around of the projector of the Darien expedition and founder of our greatest banking establishment, and attest the now indisputable place of his nativity. Patriotic individuals would be ready, and banking and commercial establishments should be ready, to add a stone to the Cairn, to supply the needful subscriptions for raising this long-deferred but richly-deserved tribute to one of Scotland's

---

* "Tell not thou star at gray daylight
   O'er Tinwald top sae bonnie o',
My footsteps 'mang the morning dew,
   When coming frae my Nannie o'."
                                    ALLAN CUNNINGHAM.

most gifted sons of the seventeenth century,—one who, amidst the distractions of that unsettled period, devoted his far-seeing genius to the cultivation of the arts of peace, with an earnestness of purpose and a success seldom or never surpassed. We have before us a printed portrait of that connexion of the family—Dr Thomas Mounsey, the Russian physician, born in the same house.* We know not, however, that any likeness of Paterson is in existence. In his days the science of photography, with which we are now familiar, was undreamt of, and portrait-painting little practised. But some appropriate monumental design may readily be selected, indicative of the genius and the adventurous spirit of the man whose memory it is intended to honour, and to hand down to future generations. *Finis coronat opus.*

* To Mr George Graham, engineer, Glasgow, a descendant of the marriage betwixt Thomas Mounsey and Janet Paterson, we are indebted for a plate of a half-length portrait of Dr Mounsey, a portly-wigged gentleman, holding in his hand " Hippocrates de Arte." The print is inscribed, "Jacobus Mounsey cæsariæ majestatis Russiæ consiliarius intimus et medicus primarius necnon cancellariæ totiusq. Facultates Medicæ per universum Imperium Archiatros et Director supremus collegii medici Regalis Edinburgensis et societates regales Londonensis, socius," &c. "Decor integer" "G. F. Schmidt. Sculpt. Regis. ad vivum fecit petrop. 1762."

THE SCOTTISH REGISTERS.

In pursuing my investigations at the General Register House in Edinburgh, respecting the genealogy of William Paterson, I had no little toil and trouble travelling to and from the metropolis. Once there, I had the freest access in this matter of public interest to the records I needed to consult. Mr William Pitt Dundas, deputy-clerk register, allowed me the land registers and Commissary records, under the superintendence of Dr Joseph Robertson, from whom I had every attention and facility. Mr George Seton, advocate, secretary, and Mr John Paton, senior clerk, kindly obliged me with the registers of births, marriages, and deaths.

The registers of births, marriages, and deaths, were instituted by the Church of Scotland in the sixteenth century, and from that remote period, down to the end of 1854, that is during nearly three centuries, they were the only acknowledged public registers for the purpose in

Scotland. The Church appointed such to be kept
in all the parishes in Scotland, nearly nine hundred in
number, the registrars being the session-clerks, acting
under the immediate oversight of the minister and elders
forming the kirk-sessions of the several parishes. The
kirk-sessions were answerable to the superior Church
Courts, Presbyteries, Synods, and General Assemblies.
There was not any compulsory registration enacted by
the state, nor penalties attached to cases of neglect. The
Church could not enforce registration, it could only
recommend it as conducive alike to public policy and
private interests. It is not to be wondered, then, that
the registrations were far from complete. Subsequent
to the severe secessions which occurred in the history
of the Church, many persons reckoned it a bondage to
acknowledge a church-officer, or apply for registration at
his hands. Nevertheless, there was a vast number of registrations under the Church and their kirk-sessions, and
when their registers came to be gathered together, down
to the end of 1819, in the new General Register House
at Edinburgh, there were found to be about three
thousand volumes of them.

When the project for a compulsory system of registration was broached in Parliament, the Church naturally
struggled to retain the registers and system of registration which she had instituted; she sought earnestly
that her registers should be allowed to continue under her
superintendence, and be made universal and compulsory.

But other influences prevailed, and, finally, on 7th August 1854, the statute, 17 and 18 of her present Majesty, cap. 80, was passed, intituled "An Act to provide for the better Registration of Births, Marriages, and Deaths in Scotland." Under the provisions of that statute, the old system of registration ceased on 31st December 1854, and the new one commenced with 1st January 1855. No longer were the registrations in the hands of the Church; no longer were they optional to parties. The registration of each individual birth, marriage, and death, was enforced under stringent penalties. The superintendence was vested in the sheriffs of counties; but under a subsequent statute, 18 and 19 Vict. cap. 29, six district examiners were appointed to oversee the registrars, and keep them strictly to the fulfilment of the important duties committed to them. Another amendment act was passed, 6th August 1860, being 23 and 24 Vict., cap. 85.

By force of these statutes, the old registers were taken from the Church,—those previous to 1820 sent to the New General Register House, Edinburgh, and those subsequent to that time transferred to the parochial registrars, whose duties commenced on 1st January 1855. In eighty-four instances, however, (which should be seen to,) the registers of parishes anterior to 1820 have not yet been transmitted, but remain with the session-clerks.

Under the new system there is this great improvement, that the registers of births, marriages, and deaths, in all the parishes in Scotland are now kept *in duplicate*, one to be retained at the registrar's office for ready reference in the locality; the other forwarded annually to the Register House, Edinburgh, for preservation and reference there. The registrars close a volume every year at 31st December; at the same time they must have an *index* made up at the end of each duplicate book, of the names contained in it, for more easy consultation. On the duplicate register books, and their duplicate indexes being compared and certified by the district examiners, one copy is sent to Edinburgh, the other retained. This plan is working admirably, and thereby we have in the parishes, and also in Edinburgh, registers of all births, marriages, and deaths, including paternity, ages, and other particulars, and the diseases and causes of death certified by the medical attendants. Mr Pitt Dundas, in his fifth report as Registrar-General, (1863,) says :—"I am happy to be able to state that the Registration Act has worked admirably in Scotland, and has amply fulfilled the ends for which it was established. I think I am justified in saying that very few births, and scarcely any deaths or marriages, which take place in Scotland, escape being entered in the public registers."

The registers so made up afford the data for the registrar-general compiling those periodical statistical returns of the rise and progress of the population, which are of the greatest interest and importance in contemplating the social edifice. In one particular, however, we think the register of deaths might be improved,—ought to be improved,—by its specifying the parish or supposed parish of the deceased's birth. Were the register to say that A. died at the age of fifty, *and was born in the parish of B.*, we could turn to the register of B. parish and learn the place and hour of A.'s birth, and obtain a key to his lineage. As the death schedule stands, we have no information whatever for tracing back the genealogy of any person dying out of the parish of his birth.

An improvement might also be made in facilitating the correction of registration errors,—for such, with all care, will now and then occur. As the law stands, errors can only be corrected by the parties concerned, and the registrars, travelling to the seat of the Sheriff Court, (however distant)—the parties to depone to the nature and cause of the errors, and the correction required, and the registrars to declare to their knowledge of the same. Now that the care of the registers is removed from the sheriffs, we think such procedure might fitly be taken before a justice of peace, in the parish or neighbourhood, or before a burgh magistrate, and reported to the district examiner. On being satisfied that the correction sought for was warranted, the district examiner at his annual supervision could attest and validate the corrected entry. There would then be no long journey to the sheriff, to deter parties and registrars from having errors corrected whenever discovered.

The taking from the functionaries of the Church of

Scotland the parochial registers of births, marriages, and deaths, preceding 1855, cannot be dispassionately regarded as other than an arbitrary act of the British Legislature. Undoubtedly it was matter of public interest that those important records should be secured in some one safe place—the General Register House at Edinburgh—both for preservation and for reference. But that might have been accomplished by making duplicates for transmission to Edinburgh, and leaving the parishes in possession of their old and much cherished records. As examples of what were torn from individual parishes, and carried to Edinburgh and retained there, the following, quoted from the new statistical account, may be given :—*Dunfermline*, (1844,) per Rev. Peter Chalmers :—"The parochial registers consist of nineteen folio volumes, the first six of which are registers of baptisms and marriages jointly ; of the remaining thirteen, nine are of baptisms, and four are of marriages. They are continuous from 16th July 1561, the date of the first entry, to the present period, excepting a blank in the marriages 1745–50. Some of the old volumes are beautifully written, and the ink is black, and still retains its shining qualities. All these registers are well bound, lettered, and dated on the back, and in good preservation." *Dumfries*, per Rev. Joseph Duncan :—"The parochial registers consist of twenty-five volumes, including the proceedings of the kirk-session. The record of baptisms commences in 1605, the marriages in 1616, and the burials in 1617 ; in all of which the entries are regular."

In justice to the whole parishes of the kingdom, excepting those who have not complied with the requirements of the statute, duplicates of the registers now held in Edinburgh ought forthwith to be made at the public expense, and sent to them. Till that be done, no one can see any parochial register preceding 1820, or obtain extract of birth, marriage, or death, unless upon going to Edinburgh, or applying there by letter. The circumstance of the registers, 1855 and downwards, being, as already mentioned, kept in duplicate, is Parliamentary acknowledgment of the principle that each locality should always have a copy of its new register. The same principle clearly demands that the parishes should have duplicates of their own preceding registers. The registrars are provided with fire-proof safes, and in their hands duplicates of the old registers, while kept secure, would be accessible to all on the spot, and give a full knowledge of the contents of each parish register, in the parish itself, from the earliest time. Compelling parties to apply to the one copy in Edinburgh, is not so satisfactory as having the register in duplicate in the parish, where it may be searched and seen by the inquirers themselves; not to speak of the serious delay, inconvenience, and expense, in going or sending to the books in Edinburgh.

Another and great advantage would be secured by having duplicates made of the old parish registers. Many of them are getting illegible through the mere lapse of time,

F

—the mouldering of the paper, and the fading of the ink. Duplicates, in good round hand, would preserve to future generations many entries which otherwise will disappear, and can never be restored.

The land registers of Scotland, commonly called the " Register of Sasines," are of the highest value in determining all questions respecting the ownership of lands and heritages ; and frequently, as we have seen, they afford irrefragable evidence in questions of genealogy which would otherwise remain for ever unsolved. They have of late had a large share of public attention. Two commissioners, Mr Charles Morton of Edinburgh, and Mr Andrew Bannatyne of Glasgow, reported upon them in 1862.* Their report led to the introduction by the Lord Advocate, into the House of Commons, 1864, of a bill for altering the system of land registration, established in 1617, and continued down to this day,—the leading principle of the bill being, that the local registers, nineteen in number, should no longer be kept in counties, or districts of counties, but be all removed to the Register House, Edinburgh, and wrought by a new staff of officials to be formed there. While such was to be the fate of the county land registers, the registers of sasines for the sixty-three Scottish royal burghs were to be continued untouched in their respective localities. This proposal to

* Report of the commissioners appointed to inquire as to the state of the registers of land rights in the counties and burghs of Scotland. Presented to Parliament 1863.

abolish the immemorial right and privilege of county local registration, and centralise all in Edinburgh, naturally occasioned much irritation over the length and breadth of Scotland; and when the second reading of the bill was moved, an opposition of a very uncompromising character broke out against it in the House. The opposition was led by Sir James Fergusson, Bart., M.P. for the county of Ayr, seconded by Mr W. E. Baxter, member for the Montrose burghs, and supported by Sir Edward Colebrooke, M.P. for Lanarkshire, Mr R. S. Aytoun of the Kirkcaldy burghs, Mr Crawford of the Ayr burghs, Mr Bouverie of the Kilmarnock burghs, Mr Dunlop of Greenock, Colonel Sykes of Aberdeen, &c. The opposition appeared to have the general support of Scotland, Edinburgh city alone excepted, whose centralising interests were represented by the Lord Advocate, Mr Mure, M.P., and Mr Adam Black. But all the eloquence of the Edinburgh gentlemen failed to convince the House, (and the counties of Scotland never will be convinced,) that transfers of lands, great or small, cannot be completed, unless by transmitting the titles to and from Edinburgh upon each transaction, for the mechanical work of registration there. The Lord Advocate yielded to the opposition, and withdrew the bill without a division; and thus the proposed measure fell to the ground.

While participating in the general satisfaction that this attempt to abolish county registration, and cen-

tralise it in Edinburgh, had such a signal discomfiture
the House of Commons, we are well persuaded that the
land registers may be improved most beneficially for the
public interest, and local registration maintained, confor-
mably alike with the feelings, the prejudices, and the
interests of the Scottish people.

We have already adverted to the benefit conferred by
the compilation and publication of the Abbreviates of
Retours down to 1700—so giving all concerned the
easiest access to them, not in Edinburgh merely, but
over Scotland. In like manner, an abridgment of the
land registers, the General and Particular Register of
Sasines, was begun at the General Register House in 1821,
—commencing, however, not with 1617, from which the
Sasine Registers date, but so late as 1781. The slow and
leisurely manner in which that work has been gone about,
and the abridgments printed, is described in the deputy-
clerk register's report, of 13th December 1864, to the
Lord Clerk Register. We thereby learn that the period
1781 to 1821 formed the first series of the abridgment,
and the period 1821-31 the second series. Of these
the indices give both the persons and places. The
third series embraced the period 1831–41; the fourth,
1841–46; the fifth, 1846–51; the sixth, 1851–61; the
seventh, embracing 1856–61, is only in progress. Of
the abridgments after 1831, the indices give the names
of persons only—not, as formerly, the names both of
persons and places. Of 1861, and following years,

the work of abridgment and indicing is not yet commenced.

The state of matters here disclosed respecting those abridgments and indices is, we think, exceedingly unsatisfactory, and indicates that there must be some heavy clogs on the wheels of Her Majesty's General Register House.

1. It seems surprising that after forty-four years' experience—from 1821 downwards—some system of abridging and indicing has not been discovered and practised, whereby the work should be accomplished more speedily, and kept short by the head. Mr Thomas Thomson in 1821 undertook the forty preceding years, — a period which required time to work up. That completed, and to which an *extra* staff might well have been applied, subsequent years ought never to have been in arrear. Yet the seventh series, 1856–61, is incomplete as regards most of Scotland; in other words, these General Register House abridgments are, at this moment, eight or nine years in arrear.

2. For the fifty years, 1781–1831, the indices gave the names both of persons and places; since 1831, the indices give only half the necessary information,—they give the names of persons but not of places. The reason assigned is, that much quicker execution of the work was expected by discontinuing the index of places. The fact, however, of the abridgments with indices of *persons* only being years in arrear, demonstrates plainly enough that those who dropped the places-index, for a great gain in celerity,

have been entirely disappointed. It is unfortunate that a discontinuance of the places-index had ever been allowed. That index is exceedingly valuable to all seeking information from the land registers. There may be numerous John Smiths (for instance) connected with lands, houses, and heritages in a county; but having his name only to refer to, the searcher must turn up and examine all the numerous references under it. After much labour he may find that not one entry in the index before him applies to the lands of John Smith of X, which are the object of the search. He must then go to other indices of names, and probably with a similar result. But, with an index of places, the searcher would at once turn up the lands of X, in the county of Y, and there he would find references to all deeds and encumbrances (if any) which affect those lands. These place-indices at once disclose the names of the successive proprietors of lands, and all their transactions respecting them, of whatever kind or character,—whether in transmissions, or feu-rights, or long tacks, or entails, or excambious, or securities, or discharges. Agreeing with those who compiled the indices, both persons and places, applicable to the retours 1560–1700, and applicable to the sasines 1781–1831, we think the indices of both should be insisted for as regards the sasine registers, ancient and modern. The deputy-clerk register, indeed, evidently leans to this same opinion, for he tells us that the discontinuance of the place-indices was pressed upon him "as a temporary measure," and he speaks of its suspension as only " for a time," adding "I have not been able, *with the limited means at my disposal,* to see my way to resuming the construction of the indices of places." Granted that there should be place-indices, the proper and convenient time for compiling them is when preparing the person-indices, having both at command, (persons and places.) Having both, searchers would have the option of referring to the one or the other, or both, according to their taste or requirements.

3. The object of those abridgments and indices, as the Report justly has it, is to make them "available to the public." Much labour has been employed in those works, and many volumes printed since 1821, but available to the public they have not been made. There has been printing but no publishing. Not a single volume of the abridgments and indices has been sent down to the district registrars for consultation in the counties. The printed volumes are withheld from the district registrars and the public, and cannot be seen or consulted unless within the dark portals of the General Register House in Edinburgh. After all the pains and expense bestowed on them, they have, under the seclusion system, proved of very little avail to the country at large.

Assuredly the country will not be satisfied with abridgments commencing only in 1781, nor with printed abridgments being locked up in Edinburgh. We would begin at the beginning, and have abbreviates of all the sasines, and other deeds appearing in them, from 1617 downwards, prepared and printed, with ample indices of names and places, and copies of them sent down to the district registrars. The minute-books, applicable to olden times, are in many instances defective—in some cases never yet made up. Nor do the old minute-book entries always set forth with sufficient clearness the persons and places contained in the deeds, of which they should be epitomes. Frequent reference must therefore be had to the volumes containing the full copies of the deeds.

Many of the olden records, both the full-length copies and the minute-books, are in good preservation and easily legible, from having been engrossed in plain round hand, with sufficiency of indelible ink on strong paper. But too frequently matters are quite different ; and what, with paper and ink wasted and faded, during two or three centuries, cramp handwriting, contracted words, and deeds in law Latin, the task of deciphering them, to ordinary readers, is equally difficult, tedious, and unsatisfactory. Use all possible pains, an unpractised hand cannot be certain that he has not misread, or altogether missed the very matter of which he was eagerly in quest. The loss of a leaf or a line, nay, the indistinctness of a single word, may frustrate the whole object of a long and laborious search. The compilation and printing of an Abbreviate of the Sasines' Registers would tend, as we suggested in reference to duplicates of the births, marriages, and deaths' registers, to preserve the essential parts of old deeds from that gradual decay into which numbers of them are now unavoidably falling.

The land registers contain much matter as well of public as of private interest, which, with the volumes, (some, of them,) almost illegible, and without a key, is practically next to useless. In their present shape they are little better than would be a handsome balance in a bank account, belonging to a party who knew not of it, or could not reach it. An abbreviate, with indices of these old registers in a good current hand, but more especially a print of them, would be of great value to the country. Many questions of property and genealogy would thereby be cleared up, which will otherwise be in doubt for ever. The same considerations which led to preparing and printing an abbreviate of the retours—shewing the ground-work of transfers of lands by *succession*—should with equal force recommend this proposal for the preparing and printing abbreviates from the sasine registers of the transfers of lands by *conveyance.*

In compiling and printing abridgments, to the limited extent above mentioned, the Register House authorities have practically acknowledged that the aid of the printing press is essential to the full development of our land registers, both ancient and modern. The cost would be small indeed, considering the free and ready and inexpensive access which would thereby be afforded to the profession and the public. If we mistake not, the fees levied in the General Register House, Edinburgh, yield a considerable yearly surplus to the public exchequer, and from that, or some other source, the necessary funds should be obtained.   One might then, by turning up the indices, gain more knowledge in a few hours of the persons and properties sought after, than he can do now in days and weeks of painful toil over the written registers.   The above remarks, we should mention, are not meant to apply to the modern land registers and their minute-books, which are kept by the registrars, under the superintendence of the Lord Clerk Register ; these are legibly written, and as easily consulted as manuscript books can be, where only one copy exists, and where that one copy is visible only during limited hours, and at one particular place.

So much for the past.   As regards the future, we would proceed in this way.   Let the registration of land rights be continued in the counties, as heretofore, same as in the burghs,—same as the registration of births, marriages, and deaths is kept locally.   Only, as is the case in the latter, the district registrars should make abridgments with indices of persons and places in duplicates, and transmit one duplicate annually to the Lord Clerk Register, to be arranged and printed—proofs being first sent to the registrars for revisal.   When thrown off, let copies be placed in the General Register House for consultation in Edinburgh, at the same time let copies be transmitted to the district registrars, in whose hands they may be consulted in the principal towns in Scotland.   At these places the public would have access to the printed abridgments for all Scotland, on payment of fees, to cover the expense, and prevent the idly curious from dipping into the affairs of others, as exhibited in these land registers. In this way, instead of dismissing county and district registrars, with or without compensation for loss of offices, these public servants would be continued, and made still more useful than they were designed to be when constituted under the Act of 1617. The General Register of Sasines, which has led to what is called the "double search," would be abolished, and all deeds or notarial instruments, applicable to a particular county, would be registered in the register for that county. So all deeds, applicable to properties in the Scottish royal burghs, come to the burghs where they respectively lie, for registration by the town-clerk in the burgh sasines' register. Where one keeper has two counties in charge, he should be required to enter their deeds in separate volumes, and make up separate minutes or abridgments, and indices. Eventually we would have a registrar resident in each county, and his register kept there, as the natural place, both for ingiving deeds and obtaining information and searches. Most counties are already provided with proper safes for keeping their land registers; those not provided would be reached by a Parliamentary enactment, such as in the Births, &c., Registration Act, as regards the parochial registers.

Those interested in holding up the General Register of

Sasines in Edinburgh, and in suppressing all the local
land registers, and drawing them within the sphere of the
Parliament House, will be ready to tell us of the difficulties—of the impossibilities—which oppose themselves to
any such improvements as we have indicated ; and of the
unspeakable advantages of sucking into Edinburgh all
the land registers of Scotland. Our answer is,—" Where
there is a will there is a way." And we are firmly
persuaded that the same pen which framed the Births,
&c., Registration Act, and continued and confirmed local
registration of these over all Scotland, without the aid of
any general register in Edinburgh, could frame an Act to
the like effect as regards our land registers. The volumes
containing the full-length copies of the deeds would,
when filled up, be transmitted, as heretofore, to the Lord
Clerk Register for preservation in Edinburgh, accompanied
by duplicate abridgments and indices for the printer.
The other duplicate would remain in the registrar's safe,
for reference in the county, without compelling people
either to go, or send to Edinburgh. The minute-books
or abridgments would give the substance of the deeds
themselves ; any one wishing to see the *ipsissima verba*
would find them, as at present, in the volumes stored at
Edinburgh. Unless in very few cases, however, the
minute-book or abridgment serves all requisite purposes,
and such in the district registrars' hands throughout
Scotland would afford every needful facility for their
consultation.

The preparations of annual indices, in alphabetical order, giving the Christian and surname of all the numerous persons who may be born, or be married, or die, within the parish or district, is required of the 901 registrars of births, &c. ; and all are duly made and transmitted to the Registrar General in Edinburgh, in reference to the registration volume of the year. In like manner, but of a much less extensive character, would be the annual indices required from the twenty or thirty registrars of land rights, along with their corresponding minute-books or abridgments. When received in January, these might be printed in February, and the proofs revised, as well in the Lord Registrar's department, as locally, and the sheets thrown off, and the volume for the preceding year put into the hands of the keepers in Edinburgh and in the county towns by March. In any of their offices we could then read in print the substance of the preceding year's land transactions, not of that county merely, but of all the counties in Scotland. To the same annual print we would add an abridgment of the year's general and special retours, also a list of adjudications and inhibitions, and generally of any other judicial steps recorded against lands or landowners during the twelve months embraced in the print.

In exemplification of the public's appreciation of local registrations, and of the accuracy and celerity with which their contents can be condensed and arranged and given out in print, we would refer to the registers of the

Scottish sheriffdoms in the matter of diligence. Of these the sheriff-clerks—officers appointed by the Crown—are the keepers, and thence, by very simple arrangements, all judicial proceedings upon dishonoured bills, decrees for debt, &c., are made known weekly by aid of the printing press, without the necessity of any private searches, such as we have in the Sasine Registers.

In times not long gone by, writs, authorising personal diligence, were not competent to the sheriff courts in Scotland. A creditor holding a bill, or a decree, against his debtor, was obliged to send his documents to Edinburgh, first for letters of horning, under the authority of the Court of Session, empowering messengers-at-arms to serve charges—requisitions for payment—on the debtors. That done, the hornings were returned to Edinburgh for captions — writs authorising the incarceration of the debtors in default of payment. The captions, when received in the county, could be used by messengers-at-arms for apprehending and incarcerating the debtors till their debts should be paid, or the creditors otherwise satisfied. A system so round about, tedious, and expensive, placed the banking and commercial and other interests over Scotland at great disadvantage, and led to a short and simple remedy. The statute 1 and 2 Vict., cap. 114, passed 1838, authorised the thirty-three sheriff courts of Scotland to issue warrants of charge and incarceration on registered protests, and decrees, of equal validity and effect as the old hornings and captions to which

Edinburgh was previously privative. Thenceforth, as the statute said, hornings and captions might be employed, but with this qualification, that no part of their cost was to be chargeable against the debtor or his estate. These writs have in consequence fallen into desuetude for ordinary purposes, and diligence is now issued in the several sheriff-courts, and executed by sheriff-officers—be the debt great or small—much more quickly and inexpensively, than under the exploded system of Edinburgh hornings and captions, executed by messengers-at-arms. This simplification-statute works admirably, and any proposal for its repeal, and a going back to Edinburgh for writs in country diligences, would receive a hasty and hearty condemnation from every district of Scotland.

The Scottish sheriff courts being thus the *loci* where early information is to be had respecting steps of diligence against debtors, it became an object with the legal and commercial interests of the country to get at that information in the speediest and most reliable manner. To this end, associations were formed, a number of years ago, for obtaining authentic particulars of all recorded protests and decrees, both in the Court of Session and in the sheriff courts. These are collected by or from the keepers week by week, arranged under the proper heads, and printed every Saturday—one of the publications being made in London, the other in Glasgow.* Thereby bankers,

* *The Mercantile Test*, London ; and *Stubbs' Weekly Gazette*, Glasgow.

lawyers, merchants, and all who desire the information, and will pay a few shillings annually for it, can have on their tables, each Monday morning, an abbreviate of the preceding week's registers of protests and decrees over all Scotland, stating the dates of the bills dishonoured, their currency, their amount, the dates of recording, the names of the acceptors or promisers, drawers and indorsers, and holders. To these are added lists of mercantile sequestrations, and of decrees in absence, issued during the week, with a summary of the gazette notices and bankruptcy proceedings touching parties whose credit or estates are there at issue. We believe the publications referred to extend also to bankruptcy proceedings in England and Ireland.

In such a task as mine has here been, the existence of printed abridgments of the land registers accessible at the county towns, would have greatly lightened my labour, and lessened its expense. Many successive journeys to Edinburgh, and days spent in the Register House, would have been saved me. Plain enough must it be to every one that a system of printed minute-books, or abridgments, of the several registers, patent to those interested, at so many registrars' offices over Scotland, would be of great practical benefit, and exceedingly popular, not with the profession merely, but with the country at large, as contrasted with the present system of having only one place — the General Register House, Edinburgh — where those registers can be got at and consulted.

For what is now proposed, no additional offices or officials would be necessary ; the county registrars would send in duplicates of their annual minute-books, and indices for the printer; the abbreviates of the other registers would be prepared by their keepers ; the salary of a superintendent in Edinburgh, and the printer's bill, would be all the cost. The registers referred to being under the authority of the Right Honourable Sir William Gibson Craig, Bart., Lord Clerk Register, the appeal lies to him, in the first instance, to take up this question of public polity, not as an Edinburgh one, but in a kindly spirit towards the country districts whose interests are deeply affected—Aberdeen, Argyle, Ayr, Banff, Berwick, Caithness, Dumbarton, Dumfries, Elgin, Fife, Forfar, Glasgow, Inverness, Kincardine, Kinross, Orkney, Perth, Renfrew, Roxburgh, Stirling, Wigtown, &c., &c. We cannot doubt the result.

The keepers of the Particular Registers of Sasines, placed at the chief towns in Scotland, hold their offices under appointments from the Crown. Generally, if not invariably, they are selected from among the practitioners before the local courts—men trained in the law and practice of conveyancing. Of such individuals no one can truly say that they are unfit for the work of registration committed to them by the Crown, or that they are not fully qualified to frame whatever abridgments or indices or duplicates may be required, under any improved or altered mode of registration. At their hands

G

full efficiency may be relied on, and having a knowledge
of the persons and places in their districts, fewer in-
accuracies will occur with them, than may be anticipated
from any new staff of officials to be got together in
Edinburgh, should such ever be sanctioned, and the immemorial system of county registration be unhappily
overthrown.

Clearly, it would be quite anomalous to allow a continuance of the burgh registers of sasines, and the
completion of transfers by registration in them as heretofore, and yet to abrogate the district registers of
sasines, (as proposed,) and deny completion to any
transfer of landward property—even though in the same
street with the burgh property—unless upon a sending of
the titles always to Edinburgh, and a registration of the
transfers by some new machinery there. When each
parish registers its own births, marriages, and deaths, and
each burgh its own land rights, why deprive the counties
of their land registers ?

It will readily be believed that the numerous practitioners in the local courts, among whom we have
the honour to rank, are by no means indifferent to
this question. They cannot be otherwise than diame-
trically opposed to the project for abolishing all the local
sasine registers, and centralising them in Edinburgh.
Their constituents, the landed proprietors in Scotland,
great and small, have found the advantage, through a
very long series of years—1617-1865—of having such

registers at their command. They have resorted to them freely : in them and in their keepers they have entire confidence. The wish and the interest of the country, undoubtedly, is to have the local registers continued— and not only continued, but rendered more generally useful than heretofore—as we think may be readily and beneficially accomplished. To the country profession the sending all writs to Edinburgh for registration would be " a heavy blow and great discouragement." It would be something like a reverting to the practice anterior to the Reform Act, when the Scottish freeholders required to go to Edinburgh with their titles for completion by Crown writs, and without which they could not claim, or be enrolled as voters. Nor should it be forgotten that the removal of the several keepers, and the discontinuance of the local registers, and supplanting them by other recipients in Edinburgh, would take away so many of the few Crown appointments to which country practitioners can aspire amid the irksome labours of ordinary professional business. We feel certain that greater utility and efficiency will be attained by maintaining the local registers, than by shutting them up and carrying the business elsewhere. We feel equally confident that the important work of registration can always be conducted in the country, where the business chiefly lies, more expeditiously and more economically, than at any centralised establishment in Edinburgh.

The public naturally look to the Lord Clerk Register,

—on the one hand, that he should lend his weighty
influence (as we feel persuaded he will do) to the placing
all the Scottish Registers on an improved footing, so
far as that can possibly be done;—on the other, that
he will dispassionately consider (and allow) the claims
of the counties to a continuation of their local registers.
His lordship has moved Government, and obtained their
sanction to the publication of several of the ancient
records of Scotland. "Hereby," as the *Courant* remarked,
"the great treasures of the Register House—the true
sources of Scottish history—will for the first time be
thrown open to the world of letters." The records so
to be brought to light are stated to be,—1st, Calendars
of the Records and State Papers of Scotland, from the
beginning of the reign of King James the Fourth, in
1488, to the union with England in 1707 ; 2d, Chronicles
and Memorials of Scotland during the Middle Ages, or
from the earliest Scottish annals to the end of the reign
of King James the Fifth, in 1542 ; and, 3d, Fac-similes
of the more interesting and important Scottish historical
documents, from the beginning of the records of Scotland,
in the eleventh century, to the union with England in the
beginning of the eighteenth. The printing and publishing of those ancient records, under the auspices of the
Lord Clerk Register, will interest chiefly the historian
and the genealogist ; the land records we would have
abridged and printed year by year would be of positive
value, not to one or two classes only, but to all engaged

in buying and selling land, or borrowing upon it—transactions of daily life.

When on this topic, we would suggest that there should be a printed catalogue of the contents of the General Register House, Edinburgh, giving a summary of the aim and object of the various records accumulated in it—the date of their institution, and whether continuous down to the present day. Therein we would include the judicial records, both civil and criminal, the parochial registers transmitted under compulsion of the Registration Act of 1854, and the records of the Church of Scotland, placed for safety in the General Register House. That printed catalogue would throw a light upon this valuable institution—the General Register House, not of Edinburgh merely, but of Scotland—which at present is veiled nearly in obscurity. One would thereby know what was to be had in this vast library—as it may be termed—what to ask for, and where in it to apply. Some of the records are for preservation only, but many of them for publication—and to all the catalogue would afford a guide never yet enjoyed.

- We would go farther ; we would also have a catalogue of all the public records in Scotland, held by counties, and burghs, (incorporations included,) and synods, and presbyteries, and kirk-sessions. These records are filled with vivid pictures of the manners and customs and wisdom of our ancestors. They are the safest guides for history, and contain reliable evidents of the patrimonial rights of

communities and individuals, ofttimes to be found nowhere else than in those records. A descriptive catalogue
of them, classified in counties, would inform all concerned
what records exist, to what periods they extend, and
where and in whose hands to be found. Moreover, the
fact of our county and town records being enumerated in
a printed catalogue would direct attention to them, and
secure their future keeping and preservation. For such
a work public money might well be applied. Or some
individual having the talent, and perseverance, and
influence, of the late Sir John Sinclair, Baronet, who
planned and accomplished the first parochial statistical
account of Scotland, might, upon his own venture, undertake and prosecute and complete the work we have indicated. All public bodies, owning records of the nature
referred to, and the custodiers of them, would, we may be
sure, lend willing hands to the compilation of a catalogue
so useful, and at the same time so truly national in its
character.

APPENDIX.

APPENDIX A.

ABRIDGMENT OF WILLIAM PATERSON'S LIFE.

WILLIAM PATERSON, the original projector of the Banks of England and of Scotland, and of the celebrated settlement of Darien, was born, it is supposed, in the year 1660, at Skipmyre, in the parish of Tinwald, Dumfries-shire. It is deeply to be regretted that no satisfactory memorials have been preserved of this remarkable man. Of his education nothing is known, but it is stated in one memoir that he was bred to the Church. He is also said to have represented the burgh of Dumfries more than once in the Scottish Parliament, and to have gone out to the West Indies in the character of a Christian missionary, where he is said to have acquired that intimate knowledge of the seas and coasts of America which led him to form the splendid idea of a settlement at Darien, by which he meant to connect the seas on the opposite sides of the globe, and to form a grand emporium of the productions of all the quarters of the earth. He returned to Europe with a scheme of trade wholly different from

the methods and principles of any of the then **trading**
companies of England, and which he was desirous of
establishing under the protection and patronage of some
European power. This scheme he seems to have laid
first before the merchants of Hamburg, afterwards before
the Dutch, and then before the elector of Brandenburg,
who all, however, received his proposals coldly. Paterson
next applied to the merchants of London, and with them
concerted the plan of the Bank of England, of which
there seems no reason to doubt that he gave the first
hint. As it has very frequently happened, however, in
similar cases, though he was admitted one of the original
directors, his richer associates no sooner became fully
possessed of his ideas, than they found out pretexts for
quarrelling with him, and finally expelled him from all
share in conducting that business of which he had been
the author. He became acquainted with Fletcher of
Salton, who had penetration enough to see and to appre-
ciate the simple splendour of his project with regard to
Darien, and patriotism enough to desire to secure the
benefits of it to his own country.

Fletcher introduced him to the Scottish administration,
and easily persuaded King William that a little more
freedom, and some new facilities of trade, would have a
happy effect. The Earl of Stair, in particular, gave the
project of Mr Paterson the support of his powerful eloquence. The result was, that an Act was passed by the
Scottish Parliament on the 26th of June 1695, "consti-
tuting John, Lord Belhaven, Adam Cockburn of Ormiston,
Lord Justice-clerk, Francis Montgomery of Giffen, Sir John
Maxwell of Pollock, Sir Robert Chiesly, present provost
of Edinburgh, John Swinton of that ilk, George Clark,
late bailie of Edinburgh, Robert Blackwood, and James

Balfour, merchants in Edinburgh; John Corse, merchant in Glasgow; WILLIAM PATERSON, Esq., James Fowlis, David Nairn, Esq., Thomas Deans, Esq., James Chiesly, John Smith, Thomas Coutes, Hugh Frazer, Joseph Cohaine, Daves Ovedo, and Walter Stuart, merchants in London, with such others as shall join with them within the space of twelve months after the first day of August next, and all others whom the foresaid persons, and those joined, or major part of them, being assembled, shall admit, and join into their joint-stock and trade, who shall all be repute as if herein originally insert, to be one body incorporate, and a free incorporation, with perpetual succession, by the name of the Company of Scotland trading to Africa and the Indies. Providing always, like as it is hereby in the first place provided, that of the fund or capital stock that shall be agreed to be advanced, and employed by the said undertakers and their copartners, the half at least shall be appointed and allotted for Scottishmen within this kingdom, who shall enter and subscribe to the said company before the first day of August 1696. And if it shall happen, that Scotsmen living within the kingdom, shall not, betwixt and the foresaid term, subscribe for, and make up the equal half of the said fund or capital stock, then, and in that case allenarly, it shall be, and is hereby allowed to Scotsmen residing abroad, or to foreigners, to come in, subscribe, and be assumed for the superplus of the said half, and no otherwise."

By the same Act the lowest subscription was fixed at one hundred pounds sterling, and the highest at three thousand. The shares of Scotsmen, too, it was provided, could be sold and alienated only to Scotsmen. The company was also vested with full powers to hold parliaments, make laws, and administer justice, &c., in any colonies they might plant; enter into treaties of peace and commerce with sovereigns, princes, estates, rulers, governors, or proprietors of lands in Asia, Africa, and America; all their ships being bound, under penalty of confiscation, to return with their cargoes in the first instance to this country, without breaking bulk by the way. They had also the exclusive privilege of trading to Asia, Africa, and America, for the period of thirty-one years; together with the free and absolute right of property to all lands, islands, colonies, cities, towns, ports, and plantations, they might come to establish or possess; paying yearly to his Majesty, and his successors in sovereignty, one hogshead of tobacco, in name of blench duty, if required. They had also the power of purchasing, for the enlargement of their trade and navigation, from foreign potentates, such exceptions, liberties, privileges, &c., as they might find convenient. Their ships were also exempted from all customs, cesses, and supplies, and their stock-in-trade from all taxes for the space of twenty-one years. All persons concerned in the company were declared denizens of the kingdom, and all persons settling in any of their colonies, cities, &c., were to be reputed natives of the kingdom, and enjoy privileges accordingly. This Act, of which the above are some of the outlines, was drawn up under the eye of Mr Paterson, and was certainly highly favourable for his purposes.

The isthmus of Darien, where there was a large tract of land bordering on both seas, the Indian and the Atlantic, which had never been in possession of any European nation, was the spot he had fixed upon for the scene of his operations, and the advantages of which he thus graphically pointed out:—"The time and expense of navigation to China, Japan, the Spice Islands, and the far greater part of the East Indies, will be lessened more than half, and the consumption of European commodities and manufactures will soon be more than doubled. Trade will increase trade, and money will beget money, and the trading world shall need no more want work for their hands, but will rather want hands for their work. Thus, this door of the seas, and key of the universe, with any-thing of a reasonable management, will, of course, enable its proprietors to give laws to both oceans, without being liable to the fatigues, expenses, and dangers, or contract-ing the guilt and blood of Alexander and Cæsar. In all our empires that have been anything universal, the con-querors have been obliged to seek out and court their conquests from afar, but the universal force and influence of this attractive magnet is such as can much more effec-tually bring empire home to the proprietors' doors. But from what hath been said, you may easily perceive that the nature of these discoveries are such as not to be en-grossed by any one nation or people with exclusion to others; nor can it be thus attempted without evident hazard and ruin, as we may see in the case of Spain and Portugal, who, by their prohibiting any other people to trade, or so much as to go to or dwell in the Indies, have not only lost their trade they were not able to maintain, but have depopulated and ruined their countries there-with, so that the Indies have rather conquered Spain and Portugal than they have conquered the Indies; for by their permitting all to go out, and none to come in, they have not only lost the people which are gone to the re-mote and luxuriant regions, but such as remain are become wholly unprofitable, and good for nothing. Thus, not unlike the case of the dog in the fable, they have lost their own countries and not gotten the Indies. People and their industry are the true riches of a prince or nation, and in respect to them all other things are but imaginary. This was well understood by the people of Rome, who, contrary to the maxims of Sparta and Spain, by general naturalisations, liberty of conscience, and immunities of government, far more effectually and advantageously conquered and kept the world than ever they did or possibly could have done by the sword."

Seeing clearly his way, Mr Paterson seems not to have had the smallest suspicion but that others would see it also, and "he makes no doubt, but that the affection we owe to our sister nation will incline the company to be zealous in using all becoming endeavours for bringing our fellow-subjects to be jointly concerned in this great, extensive, and advantageous undertaking. That a proposal of this kind from the company will be other than acceptable ought not to be supposed, since by this means the consumption and demand of English manufactures, and consequently the employment of their people, will soon be more than doubled. England will be hereby enabled to become the long-desired seaport, and yet its public revenues, instead of being diminished, will thereby be greatly increased. By this their nation will at once be eased of its laws of restraint and prohibitions, which, instead of being encouragements, always have, and still continue to be, the greatest lets to its trade and happiness."

These enlightened views seem to have made a greater impression on the public mind than at that time could have been anticipated. In the month of October 1695, Lord Belhaven, Mr Robert Blackwood, and Mr James Balfour, went on a deputation to London, accompanied by Mr Paterson, where the subscription books were first opened, and in the course of nine days three hundred thousand pounds were subscribed ; one-fourth of all subscriptions being paid in cash. This promising state of things, however, was, by the jealousy of the English monopolists, suddenly reversed.

The English Parliament, with a spirit worthy of the darkest ages and the most barbarous nations, declared Lord Belhaven, William Paterson, and the other members of the deputation, guilty of a high crime and misdemeanour, for administering in that kingdom the oath *de fideli* to a foreign association. Those of the English people who had become partners in the company were threatened with an impeachment, and were by this means compelled to withdraw their subscriptions. The company was left to the unassisted resources of their own poor and depressed country. The eagerness with which the scheme had been patronised abroad by wealthy individuals, and the bitterness of the opposition directed against it by the Government of England, equally tended to give it importance in the eyes of Scotsmen. Nothing could exceed the eagerness with which all classes of the Scottish people hastened to enrol themselves in the magnificent copartnery now forming. Every burgh, every city, and almost every family of any consequence, became shareholders. Four hundred thousand pounds were subscribed ; an astonishing sum when it is known, that at that time the circulating capital of the kingdom did not exceed eight hundred thousand pounds sterling. To this enthusiasm a variety of causes contributed. The scheme of Paterson was politically good. It was drawn up with great ability, and promised important results in a moral and religious, as well as in a commercial, point of view. The scene of the intended operations became the subject of numberless pamphlets, wherein fancy was much more largely employed than fact. The soil was represented as rich, and teeming with the most luxuriant fertility; the rivers, as full of fish, and their sands sparkling with gold; the woods smiling in perpetual verdure, at all times ringing with the melody of spring, and loading every breeze that swept over them with the most delightful odours.

Having completed their preparations, the colony, in presence of the whole city of Edinburgh, which poured out its inhabitants to witness the scene, embarked; Mr Paterson going first on board at Leith, from the roads of which they sailed on the 26th of July 1698. The fleet consisted of five ships purchased at Hamburg or Holland—for they were refused even the trifling accommodation of a ship of war which was laid up at Burntisland—and were named the *Caledonia, St Andrew, Unicorn, Dolphin*, and *Endeavour;* the two last being yachts laden with provisions and military stores. The colony consisted of twelve hundred men; three hundred of them being young men of the best Scottish families. Among them were also sixty officers who had been thrown out of employment by the peace which had just been concluded, and who carried along with them the troops they had commanded; all of whom were men who had been raised on their own estates, or on those of their relations. Many soldiers and sailors, whose services had been refused—for many more than could be employed had offered themselves—were found hid in the ships, and when ordered ashore, clung to the ropes imploring to be allowed to go with their countrymen without fee or reward. The whole sailed amidst the praises, the prayers, and the tears of relations, friends, and countrymen; "and neighbouring nations," says Dalrymple, "saw with a mixture of surprise and respect the poorest nation of Europe sending forth the most gallant colony which had ever gone from the old to the new world."

The colony, on 3d November 1698, landed between Portobello and Carthagena at a place called Acta, where there was an excellent harbour, about four miles from Golden Island. Having obtained the sanction of the natives to settle among them, they proceeded to cut through a peninsula, by which they obtained what they conceived to be a favourable site for a city, and they accordingly began to build one under the name of New Edinburgh. They also constructed a fort in a commanding situation for the protection of the town and the harbour, which they named St Andrew; and on the country itself they imposed the name of Caledonia.

The first care of the council, which had been appointed by the company, and of which Mr Paterson was one of the chief, was to establish a friendly correspondence with the native chiefs. On the 28th of December 1698, the council issued a proclamation dated at New Edinburgh, to the following effect :—" We do hereby publish and declare, That all manner of persons, of what nation or people soever, are and shall from henceforward be equally free, and alike capable of the said properties, privileges, protections, immunities, and rights of government, granted unto us; and the merchants and merchant ships of all nations may freely come to and trade with us without being liable in their persons or goods to any manner of capture, confiscation, seizure, forfeiture, attachment, arrest, restraint, or prohibition for, or by reason of any embargo, breach of the peace, letters of marque, or reprisals, declaration of war with any foreign prince, potentate, or state, or upon any other account or pretence whatsoever. And we do hereby not only grant, concede, and declare, a

general and equal freedom of government and trade to
those of all nations who shall hereafter be of or concerned
with us ; but also, a full and free liberty of conscience in
matters of religion, so as the same be not understood to
allow, connive at, or indulge, the blaspheming of God's
holy name, or any of His divine attributes, or of the un-
hallowing or profaning the Sabbath-day ; and, finally, as
the best and surest means to render any government successful, durable, and happy, it shall, by the help of Almighty God, be ever our constant and chiefest care, that
all our further constitutions, laws, and ordinances be con-
sonant and agreeable to the holy Scriptures, right reason,
and the examples of the wisest and justest nations ; that
from the righteousness thereof we may reasonably hope
for and expect the blessings of prosperity and increase."
A parliament was formed, which held at least two ses-
sions. In April 1699, it enacted thirty-four statutes for
the regulation of civil and criminal justice in the colony.
Several items bear strong marks of the liberal spirit and
philosophic mind of Paterson.

Mr Paterson had taken the precaution to land his people
at the beginning of winter, the best season for Europeans
encountering the climate of Darien ; and the first letter
from the council to the directors thus expressed the satisfaction of the colonists with their new destination :—" As
to the country, we find it very healthful ; for, though we
arrived here in the rainy season, from which we had little
or no shelter for several weeks together, and many sick
among us, yet we are so far recovered, and in so good a
state of health, as could hardly anywhere be expected
among such a number of men together. In fruitfulness,
this country seems not to give place to any in the world ;
for we have seen several of the fruits, as cocoa-nuts, bar-

illas, sugar-canes, maize, oranges, &c., &c., all of them, in
their kinds, the best anywhere to be found. Nay, there
is hardly a foot of ground but may be cultivated; for
even upon the very tops and sides of the hills, there is
commonly three or four feet deep of rich earth, without
so much as a stone to be found therein. Here is good
hunting, and fowling, and excellent fishing in the bays
and creeks of the coast; so that, could we improve the
season of the year just now begun, we should soon be
able to subsist of ourselves; but building and fortify-
ing will lose us a whole year's planting."

This was no more than all of them must have foreseen;
and they never doubted of obtaining more provisions than
they could want, from the West India islands, or from
the American colonies. Unfortunately, orders were sent
out after them to all English governors, prohibiting com-
munication with them. These proclamations were rigidly
adhered to, and the unfortunate Scottish colonists were
denied those supplies which had seldom been withheld
from lawless smugglers, bucaniers, and pirates. The
colony had to be put on short allowance, when the sickly
season was thinning their numbers, and bringing additional duty on those who were in health. In this emer-
gency, their Indian friends exerted themselves on their
behalf, putting to shame their Christian brethren, who,
from a mean jealousy, were attempting to starve them;
and they might still have done better, had not insubordi-
nation broken out among themselves, and a conspiracy
been formed, in which some of the council were impli-
cated, to seize one of the vessels, and to make their escape
from the colony.

After matters had come this length, Paterson succeeded
in assuming new councillors; a measure which had the

H

effect of checking the turbulence of the discontented.
The new council also despatched one of their own number to Britain, with an address to the king, and a pressing
request to send them out supplies of provisions, ammunition, and men.   On receiving this despatch, the directors
lost no time in sending out the requisite supplies.   They
had already sent despatches and provisions by a brig
which sailed from the Clyde in the end of February 1699,
but which unhappily never reached her destination.   The
Olive Branch, Captain Jamieson, and another vessel, with
three hundred recruits and store of provisions, arms and
ammunition, were despatched from Leith roads on the
12th of May 1699.   Matters in the colony were in the
meantime getting worse; and on the 22d of June, they
came to the resolution of abandoning the place within
eight months of the time they had taken possession of it.
The unfortunate projector himself was at the time on
board the *Union*, whither he had been conveyed some
days before in a fever, brought on by anxiety and grief
for the weakness of his colleagues, and the frustration of
those hopes which he had so sanguinely cherished, and
which he had found so nearly realised.   He, however, recovered at New York, whence he returned to Scotland, to
make his report to the company.

A fleet of four ships, the *Rising Sun*, *Hope*, *Duke
Hamilton*, and *Hope of Borrowstowness*, with thirteen
hundred men, sailed from the Isle of Bute, on the 24th
of September 1699, and reached Caledonia Bay on
the 30th of November following.   Everything, however,
went against them.   Having arrived in the harbour of
New Edinburgh, the recruits by the *Olive Branch* and
her consort determined to land, and repossess themselves of the place, the huts of which they found burnt

down, and totally deserted. One of the ships, however, took fire, and was burnt in the harbour; the others set sail for Jamaica. When the fleet which followed arrived in November, and, instead of a colony ready to receive them, found the huts burnt down, the forts dismantled, and the ground which had been cleared overgrown with shrubs and weeds, with all the tools and implements of husbandry taken away, they were at a loss what to do.

Two ministers, Messrs James and Scott, went out with the first expedition, but the one died on the passage, and the other shortly after landing in New Caledonia. The council having written home to the directors, regretting the death of their ministers, and begging that others might be sent to supply their place, the commission of the General Assembly of the Church of Scotland, at the particular desire of the board of directors, sent out the reverend Messrs Alexander Shields, (the well-known author of the " Hind let Loose," "Life of Renwick," &c.,) Borland, Stobo, and Dalgliesh. These persons sailed in the last fleet. The Church of Scotland took a deep interest in the colony of Darien, and sent a particular admonition by the ministers, of which the following may be taken as a specimen :—" We shall, in the next place, particularly address ourselves to you that are in military charge and have command over the soldiery, whether by land or sea. It is on you, honoured and worthy gentlemen, that a great share of the burden of the public safety lies. You are, in some respects, both the hands and the eyes of this infant colony. Many of you have lately been engaged in a just and glorious war, for retrieving and defending the Protestant religion, the liberties and rights of your country, under the conduct of a matchless prince.

And now, when, through the blessing of the Lord of
hosts, His and your arms have procured an honourable
peace at home; you, and others with you, have, with
much bravery, embarked yourselves in a great, generous,
and just undertaking, in the remote parts of the earth,
for advancing the honour and interest of your native
country. If in this you acquit yourselves like men and
Christians, your fame will be renowned both abroad and
at home."

Alarmed by the accounts which they soon after received
from Darien, the council-general of the company despatched a proclamation, declaring " that it shall be lawful
to any person of whatever degree inhabiting the colony,
not only to protest against, but to disobey, and oppose
any resolution to desert the colony;" and, " that it shall
be death, either publicly or privately, to move, deliberate,
or reason upon any such desertion or surrender, without
special order from the council-general for that effect.
And they order and require the council of Caledonia to
proclaim this solemnly, as they shall be answerable."
Before this act was passed in Edinburgh, however, New
Caledonia was once more evacuated. The inhabitants of
the colony having gone on shipboard, with all that belonged to them, they weighed anchor on the 11th of April
1700, and sailed for Jamaica, after having occupied New
Caledonia somewhat more than four months. The *Hope,*
on board of which was Captain Veitch, and the greater
part of the property, was wrecked on the rocks of Colo-
rades, on the western coast of Cuba. The *Rising Sun* was
wrecked on the bar of Carolina, and the captain and crew,
with the exception of sixteen persons who had previously
landed, were lost. Of the few survivors, some remained

in the English settlements, some died in Spanish prisons; and of the three thousand men that at different periods went out to the settlement, perhaps not above twenty ever regained their native land.

In this melancholy manner terminated the only attempt at colonisation ever made by Scotland. That it was an attempt far beyond the means of the nation, must be admitted. The conception, however, was splendid, the promise great, and every way worthy of the experiment; and but for the jealousy of the English and the Dutch, more particularly the former, might possibly have succeeded. Had the wants of the Scottish settlers been supplied by the English colonies, which they could very well have been, the first and most fatal disunion, and abandonment of their station, could not have happened; and had they been acknowledged by their sovereign, the attack made upon them by the Spaniards, which put an end to the colony, would never have been made. Time would have smoothed down the asperities among the settlers themselves; experience would have corrected their errors in legislation; and New Caledonia, which remains to this day a wilderness, might have become the emporium of half the commerce of the world.

Mr Paterson died at an advanced age. After the Union, he claimed upon the Equivalent Money for the losses he had sustained at Darien, and none had a fairer claim. But he never received one farthing. Had Paterson's scheme succeeded, and it was no fault of his that it did not, his name had unquestionably been enrolled among the most illustrious benefactors of his species. There is one part of his character which, in a man of so much genius, ought not to pass unnoticed: "He was void of

passion; and he was one of the very few of his countrymen who never drank wine." *

APPENDIX B.

INSTRUMENT OF SASINE IN FAVOUR OF JOHN PATERSON,
YR OF KINHARVEY, FROM PARTICULAR REGISTER OF
SASINES KEPT AT DUMFRIES, FOR THE COUNTY OF
DUMFRIES AND STEWARTRY OF KIRKCUDBRIGHT.

At Dumfries, the thirty ane day of May, Jaivy and ane
years, (1701,) the qlk day, the seasine underwritten was
presented by Robert Edgar, wrytter yʳ, to be reg'rat, qʳof
the tenor follows : In the name of God, amen. To all and
sundrie whom it may concerne, be this present publick
instrument, be it known that upon the twenty second
day of Apryl, Jaivy and ane years, and of the regne of
our Sovereign Lord William, by the grace of God King
of Great Britain, France, and Ireland, defender of the
faith, the threttein year—In pre'ce of me Nottar Publick,
and witnesses under subscryveing, compᵈ personallie,
upon the ground of the lands of Kinharvie, *alias* Clocklowie after mentioned, ane discreet man, John Patersone
of Kenhervie, granter of the obligement and precept of
seasine contained in the contract of marriage, after
specᵗ, to the effect underwryten. And upon the said
lands compᵈ also persllʸ John Patersone, eldest lawful son to the said John Patersone of Kenharvie, having

* Abridged, with permission of Messrs Blackie & Son of Glasgow,
the publishers, from Dr Robert Chambers's Scottish Biographical
Dictionary, edition 1834.

and holding in his hands the contract of marriage, past
and ended betwixt him, with consent of his said father
and Bethia Patersone, lau[ll] daughter to the s[d] John Patersone in Skipmyre, with consent of her said father, and
taking burden on him for her on the one and oy'r pts. of
the dait, the nynten day of March last past.   By which
contract, in contemplation of the marriage then contracted and y[r]after solemnized betwixt the sd[s] parties,
the said John Patersone, elder, of Kenharvie, bound and
obliged him and his aires, with all convenient diligence,
duly and lau'lly to infeft and seize ye s[d] John Patersone,
his sone and his aires, and successors q[t]somever, herita-
blie and irredeemablie, in all and haill his fourtie
shilling land of Kenharvie, *alias* Clocklowie, with houses,
biggings, yards, orchards, mosses, muirs, meadows, common pasturages, pts., pendicles, and pertinents of the
samen lying within the parish of Newabay, and Stewart-
rie of Kirkcudbright, and thereby reservit to himself
and Margaret Affleck his spous, and the survivor of them,
y[r] liferent and conjunct fee right of the saids lands
during y[r] lyfetimes, to be holden either of him or from
him of his immediate superiors, in maner y[r]in ment[d],
by resignation or confirmation at the option of the said
John Patersone, younger, as the s[d] contract contains
pro'rie of resignation in his favor, clause of absolute
warranthie, and ane precept of seasine of the sd[s] lands
also in his favors, p. ports : Q'ch contract containing
the said obligement for infeftment and precept of seasine,
the said John Patersone, younger, did exhibit and present
to the s[d] John Patersone his father, desiring and requir-
ing him, for the due implement of the said obligement to
infeft, and of the said precept of seasine granted for that
effect after the forme and tenor y[r]of.   And the said

John Patersone, elder, being willing to obtemper and fulfil his obligement, accordingly did receive the said contract of marriage in his hands, and delivered it to me notar publick, in order to overreading y^{r}of, and the s^d obligement and precept of seasine y^{r}in contained, in audience of the witness undernamed by standing : Q'lk contract I took and he performed, and immediately y^{r}after the said John Patersone, elder, of Kenharvie, for the due implement and performance of the above wr'tn obligement for infeftment foresaid, contained in the said contract of · marriage, and in supplement of the said precept of seasine granted by him y^{r}anent, also y^{r}n comprehended, *propriis manibus,* gave and delivered stait and seasine with actual, real, and corporal possession to the s^d John Patersone, younger, and his foresaids, heritably and irredeemably, of all and hail the afores^{ds} fourtie shilling land of Kinharvie, *alias* Clocklowie, with houses, biggings, yards, orchards, mosses, muirs, meadows, common pasturages, pts., pendicles, and pertinents of the samen lying as s^d is, reserving always to the said John Patersone himself, and Margaret Afflek, his spouse. and the survivor of them, y^r liferent and conjunct fee right of the sd^s lands during her lifetime. Be delivery of earth and stone of the ground of the sd^s lands, as use is, in the hands of the s^d John Patersone, younger, present accepting and receiving the same, to be holden either of the s^d John Patersone, elder, himself in free blench, as s^d is, or from him of his immediate lawful superiors of s^{d}s lands, after the form and tenor of the said obligement to infeft and precept of Seasine containt in the s^d contract of marriage in all poynts. Whereupon and upon the hail premises, the said John Patersone y^r, of me notar publick undersubscribing, asked and required instruments ane or mae, as many as were needful. And this was done upon the ground of the sd⁴ lands of Kenharvie, *alias* Clocklowie, betwixt the hours of three and four or yʳby, in the afternoon of the day, month, year, and regne @ set down, in presence of Thomas Muncie, in Skip-myre ; James Patersone in Cullencleugh ; James Pater-son, second lawful son to the said John Patersone, elder ; and Wm. Muncie, son to the said Thomas Muncie, witnesses specially called and required to the premises. (*Follows notary's docquet.*) *Sic Subscribuntur*—Regnum immortale petendum—ROBT. EDGAR, *N. P.* THOMAS MUNCIE, *witness.*   JAMES PATERSONE, *witness.*   JAMES PATERSONE, *witness.*   WILLIAM MUNCIE, *witness.*   Regᵈ, JO. SHARP.

APPENDIX C.

INSTRUMENT OF SASINE IN FAVOUR OF MRS BETHIA PATER-SON, SPOUSE OF JOHN PATERSON, YOUNGER, OF KIN-HARVEY, FROM THE PARTICULAR REGISTER OF SASINES KEPT AT DUMFRIES FOR THE COUNTY OF DUMFRIES AND STEWARTRY OF KIRKCUDBRIGHT.

AT Dumfries, the thirty-ane day of May, 1701 years, whilk day the sasine underwritten was presented by Robert Edgar, writer there, to be registered, whereof the tenor follows : In the name of God, Amen. To all and sundrie whom it may concern, be this present public in-strument, be it known that upon the 22d day of April, 1701 years, and of the reign of our sovereign Lord William, by the grace of God king of Great Britain,

France, and Ireland, defender of the faith, the thirteen year, in presence of me notar public and witnesses under subscribing, compeared personally, upon the ground of the lands of Kenharvie, *alias* Clocklowie, John Paterson, eldest lawful son to John Paterson of Kenharvie, granter of the obligement and precept of sasine contained in the contract of marriage underwritten to the effect after exprest, and thereupon with him compeiret also personally, Bethia Patersone, his spouse, lawful daughter to John Patersone of Skipmyre, having and holding in his hands the contract of marriage made and ended betwixt the said John Paterson, younger, with consent of his said father, and the said Bethia with consent of her said father, and taking burden on him for her on the ane and other parts of the date, the nineteen day of March last by past. By whilk contract for the marriage then treated and thereafter solemnizit betwixt the saids parties, the said John Patersone, younger, bound and obliged him and his aires and successors duly and lawfully to infeft and seise the said Bethia Patersone, then his affidat spouse, in liferent enduring all the days of her lifetime in case of her survivance of her said husband, in ane an. rent or annuitie of fourtie pound Scots money, free of all teinds, stipend, schoolmaster's fees, cesses, and other public burdens and exactions whatsomever, yearly, at Whitsunday and Martinmas, by equal portions, to be uplifted forth of All and Haill the fourtie shilling land of Kinharvie, *alias* Clocklowie, with houses, biggings, yards, parts, pendicles, and pertinents thereof, lying within the parish of Newabbey, and stewartry of Kirkcudbright, or furth of any part or portion, first, best, and readiest of the mails, rents, profits, and duties of the saids lands, beginning the first payment, &c.; and it is by the

said contract provided and declared, that the foresaid
liferent annuitie shall be without prejudice to the said
Bethia Patersone of ane farther additional liferent annuitie
and provision corresponding and suitable to the value of
the moveable goods, gear, and others which are thereby
assignit in favors of him and his said spouse, by the said
John Paterson *in* Skipmyre, and which shall acress to
them at his decease, under reservation of Bethia Patersone,
spouse to the said John Paterson, elder, hir just third
part and share thereof, and for whilk additional liferent
provisions accordingly the said John Patersone stands
bound and obliged,* and to grant, in favors of his said
spouse, all writs and securities thereupon for her said liferent in case of her survivance as said is, as the said contract of marriage, containing procuratorie of resignation,
clause of absolute warrandice, and ane precept of sasine
of the said annual rent in favor of the said Bethia Patersone, effeirs ; the qlk contract of marriage containing the
said obligement for infeftment and precept of sasine, the
said Bethia Patersone did exhibit and present to the said
John Patersone younger, her husband, desiring and re-
quiring him, for the due implement of his said obligement to infeft, and of the said precept of sasine granted
for that effect after the form and tenor thereof. (Here
follow the formal clauses, specifying delivery of sasine
by John Paterson the younger, to his said spouse, of the
foresaid lands in security of said annual rent; but the

* This clause imports that Bethia the daughter, was to get from
her father's means a liferent annuity corresponding to certain
moveable goods, gear, and others assigned by some clause in the
marriage-contract not copied into the sasine,—under reservation,
however, of Bethia the mother's one third thereof, for which her
husband, Skipmyre, stood bound probably in a contract or ante-
nuptial marriage-contract betwixt themselves.

precept of sasine and testing clause of the contract are not engrossed.) And this was done upon the ground of the said lands of Kinharvie, *alias* Clocklowie, betwixt the hours of three and four or thereby in the afternoon of the day, month, year, and reign above written. In presence of Thomas Muncie in Skipmyre, James Patersone in Cullencleugh, James Patersone, second lawful sone to the said John Patersone, elder of Kenharvie, and William Muncie, sone to the said Thomas Muncie, witnesses speciallie called and required to the premises. (*Then follows notary's Latin docquet.*) (Signed,)—*Regnum immortale petendum*—R. E., *N. P.* THOMAS MUNCIE, *witness.* JAMES PATERSONE, *witness.* JAMES PATERSON, *witness.* WILLIAM MUNCIE, *witness.* JO. SHARP, *Keeper of Register.*

APPENDIX D.

DR CARLYLE ON TINWALD MANSE ECONOMY.

Of Mr Robison and his wife and family and their economy at Tinwald manse, Dr Carlyle says,—" Mr Robison had been minister at Tinwald since the year 1697, and was a member of the commission which sat during the Union Parliament. He was a man of a sound head, and in the midst of very warm times was resorted to by both laity and clergy for temperate and sound advice. He lived to the year 1761, and I passed several summers and one winter entirely, at his house, when a student. . . . His wife, Jean Graham, connected with many of the principal families in Galloway, and descended by her mother from the Queensberry family, (as my father was at a greater distance by his mother, of the Jardine Hall family,) gave the worthy people and their children an air of greater consequence than their neighbours of the same rank, and tended to make them deserve the respect which was shown them. When I look back on the fulness of very good living to their numerous family, and to their cheerful hospitality to strangers—when I recollect the decent education they gave their children, and how happily the daughters were settled in the world ; and recollect that they had not £70 per annum, besides the £500 which was my grandmother's portion,—it appears quite surprising how it was possible for them to live as they did, and keep their credit. What I have seen, both at their house and my father's on their slender incomes, surpasses all belief. But it was wonderful what moderation and a strict economy was able to do in those days."

APPENDIX E.

JOHN CUNNINGHAM AND HIS FAMILY.

JOHN CUNNINGHAM, my maternal grandfather, (son of James Cunningham, farmer at Gogar-Mains, a few miles west of Edinburgh, and Mary Aitchison of the parish of Chirnside, his spouse,) was in Dr Mounsey's service at Rammerscales, and assisted in his estate improvements. He married Elizabeth Harley of Dumfries, and they had nine children, five sons and four daughters, of whom my mother was the eldest. He became tenant of the farm of Culfad, in the parish of Kirkpatrick-Durham, stewartry

of Kirkcudbright, and finally settled at Dalswinton, near
Dumfries, as land steward to the late Mr Patrick Millar
of Dalswinton. In the end of the last century and beginning of this, Mr Millar, as is well known, was one of the
foremost Scottish agriculturists, and at the same time,
renowned in the scientific world as the earliest, or one of
the earliest, promoters of steam navigation in Britain.
When about Dalswinton in 1811–12, I recollect some of
Mr Millar's paddle boats, for driving by the hand, lying
on the loch. Burns farmed Ellisland on Dalswinton
estate, and he and my grandfather were on intimate
terms down to the poet's death at Dumfries on 21st July
1796. Cunningham died in Mr Millar's service at Dalswinton in 1800. His widow, my grandmother, survived
till 22d February 1845, when she died at the great age
of ninety-five. How their children took a liking to letters
does not appear. But though not authors by profession,—in those days, indeed, there was comparatively
little encouragement for such,—several of them found
leisure, amid their other engagements, to make considerable contributions to literature.

The eldest son, *James,* mason at Dalswinton village,
was deeply read in the history and antiquities of his
country, and wrote occasionally for the periodical press.

The second son, *Thomas Mouncey Cunningham*—named
after Dr Mounsey—was born at Culfad, in the Stewartry,
25th June 1776, turned his attention to mechanics, and
died at London, 28th October 1834, in the service of
Rennie, the celebrated engineer, where he was long chief
clerk. He wrote a good deal, both in prose and poetry,
in the beginning of this century ; and a number of his
pieces are to be found in the Scottish magazines of the
day. His ardent attachment to the people of his native

Galloway, and its hills and dales, is recorded to latest posterity in his popular song, "The Hills of Galloway."

The numerous prose and poetic works of his younger brother, *Allan Cunningham*, and Allan's connexion with Sir Francis Chantrey the sculptor, are well known. Born at Blackwood, parish of Keir, Dumfriesshire, 7th December 1784, Allan died in London, 29th October 1842, in the height of his fame. His grave, in the general cemetery at Kensal Green, is marked by a stone of solid granite, erected by his widow and five then surviving children. Mrs Cunningham outlived her husband till a recent date, 8th September 1864. My uncle had an invitation in 1831 from Mr and Mrs Macalpine Leny of Dalswinton, to forsake the bustle of the metropolis, and spend the evening of his days on the banks of his native Nith, where they would find him "a cot, a kale-yard, and a cow."* But it was not ordered he should enjoy that enviable retirement. When reviving, one sunny afternoon, middle of last August, (1864,) my juvenile recollections of Dalswinton, and the ancient castle of the Comyns, and the heronry, and stately swans, and fertile holms, Mrs Leny pointed out the intended cottage site had my uncle closed with the invitation referred to. The spot is a lovely one, in a sheltered glen near Crofthead, on Dalswinton estate —just such a place as a poet's soul might yearn for :—

> " Dalswintonhill, Dalswintonholm,
> And Nith, thou gentle river,
> Rise in my heart, flow in my soul,
> And dwell with me forever ! "

The youngest son, *Peter Cunningham*, died at Green-

* Poems and Songs, by Allan Cunningham ; edited by his son, Peter Cunningham. London : John Murray, 1847.

wich, 6th March 1864, and rests in the Nunhead Cemetery near London. The *Gentleman's Magazine*, June 1864, in recording his death, said :—The deceased, who was the younger brother of Thomas Mounsey Cunningham, (a well-known name in Scottish provincial literature,) and of Allan Cunningham, was born at Dalswinton in Dumfriesshire, on 14th November 1789, and received his baptismal name from that Peter Millar who is generally recognised as the first person to make use of steam in propelling boats. He received his medical education at the University of Edinburgh, and so soon as he attained the requisite age, was appointed an assistant surgeon in the Royal Navy. In this capacity he saw service on the shores of Spain, when the great war was raging, and on the Lakes of America, where he became the close friend of the celebrated Clapperton. He also served for some years in the Eastern Archipelago, and had ample opportunities of observing the effect of tropical climates on the European constitution. Of this he profited, when, peace having arrived, he was thrown out of the regular line of duty, and would have been left to vegetate on half-pay had he not sought other employment from the Admiralty, in the course of which—to use the words of the *Quarterly Review*—he " made no less than four voyages to New South Wales, as surgeon-superintendent of convict ships, in which were transported upwards of six hundred convicts of both sexes, whom he saw landed at Sidney without the loss of a single individual, a fact of itself quite sufficient to attest his judgment and ability in the treatment and management of a set of beings not easily kept in order."—*Q. R., Jan.* 1828. The result of his observations during this period was embodied in his " Two Years in New South Wales," which was published in 1827 in

two volumes, post 8vo, and rapidly ran through three
large editions. This book is both amusing and instructive, and though necessarily superseded by more recent
works on the same ever-extending subject, is still frequently quoted, and some centuries hence will afford a
mine of information and speculation to the correspon-
dents of the *sylvanus urban* of the Antipodes. Mr Cunningham added the profits of this work to his early
savings in the navy, and expended them in an attempt to
open up a large tract of land, (on Hunter's River, named
by him Dalswinton, after his birthplace,) in what he then
fondly regarded as his adopted country. But the locality
was perhaps badly chosen, the seasons unpropitious, and
he soon abandoned the struggle so far as his own personal
superintendence was concerned. His well-earned reputa-
tion, however, at the Admiralty speedily procured him
employment, and he served successively in the *Tyne*, 18,
on the South American station, and in the *Asia*, 84, in the
Mediterranean. In the course of these years he published
a volume of "Essays on Electricity and Magnetism," and
another on "Irrigation, as Practised on the Eastern Shores
of the Mediterranean." He also contributed "An Account
of a Visit to the Falkland Islands" to the *Athenæum*, and
was a frequent writer in other periodicals. He was a man
of remarkable powers of observation, and of the most
amiable and conciliatory disposition ; and, it is believed,
passed through life without making a single enemy. His
attachment to his brother Allan was particularly strong,
and although death had separated them for more than
twenty years, the name of that brother was among the
last articulate sounds which passed his lips. It was well
remarked by the *Quarterly Review* in the article before
quoted, that the appearance of two such men—(the re-

I

viewer might have said *four* such sons)—in one humble-bred cottage family is a circumstance of which their country has reason to be proud.

Excepting the quotation now made, I had the above information chiefly from my aunt, Miss Wilhelmina Cunningham of Dumfries, the only surviving child of John Cunningham, and from whom, also, I learned that the late Honourable Lord Cunningham, one of the Lords of Session in Scotland, and of Duloch, Fifeshire, was of the same Gogar-mains family.

APPENDIX F.

THE DARIEN HOUSE.

AMONG the relics in Edinburgh of Paterson's ill-fated expedition, may be seen the building erected in the city for carrying on the Darièn Company's business, and accommodating their officials; for counting, we may suppose, the inordinate gains expected from the enterprise, and 'preserving to future generations the history and books and muniments of that great scheme. But while man proposes God disposes; and the mansion vainly designed for a receptacle of untold wealth, was doomed soon to become no other than an abode for squalid poverty. We have the following account of the building in "Wilson's Memorials of Edinburgh," vol. i., p. 106. 1848 :—

"The old Darien house still stands within the extended line of the city wall, near the Bristo Port, a melancholy and desolate-looking memorial of that unfortunate enterprise. It is a substantial and somewhat handsome structure, in the French style, and with the curious high pitched roof which prevailed in the reign of William III. It has

more recently been abandoned to the purposes of a pauper
lunatic asylum, and is popularly known by the name of
Bedlam. A melancholy association attaches to a more
modern portion of it, towards the south, as having been
the scene where poor Ferguson, that unhappy child of
genius, so wretchedly terminated his brief career. The
building bears on an ornamental tablet above the main
entrance, the date 1698, surmounted by a sun dial. The
only relic of its original grandeur that has survived its
adaptation to later purposes, is a handsome and very substantial stone balustrade, which guards the broad flight
of steps leading to the first floor."

A woodcut of the building is subjoined to the above
account of it in Mr Wilson's volume.

APPENDIX G.

THE ORIGIN OF THE NAME "PAGAN" AS APPLIED TO INDI-VIDUAL FAMILIES.

Like many other persons, I was early indoctrinated in
the belief that those acknowledging the Pagan name had
received it through their being descended of the ancient heathens or idolaters. But when a student at the
University of Edinburgh, Mr David Laing, whose acquain-
tance I gained through my late uncle Allan Cunningham,
kindly and considerately complimented me with a couple
of volumes which told that that family name had quite
a different origin,—that it was given in the days of the
crusades to warriors from different countries who had
distinguished themselves in combats against the pagans
or infidels. So the renowned Publius Cornelius Scipio
was surnamed "Africanus," from his having carried the

war betwixt Rome and Carthage into Africa, and there
conquered the Carthaginians.

One of the volumes I had (and have) from Mr Laing,
was "Relation historique et geographique, de la grande
Riviere des Amazones, dans l'Amerique, par le compte
de Pagan. Avec la carte d'icelle rivier, et de ses provinces.
A Paris, 1655." The other was an English translation of
the same work by William Hamilton, dedicated by him
"to the imperial majesty of Charles II. of Great Britain,
France, and Ireland, Defender of the Faith of Protestants,
and of Protestants themselves, by his title of signal pro-
vidence, happiness, victories, triumphs." The translation
was printed at London, "by John Starkey, at the Miter in
Fleet Street, near Templebarre, 1661." In his royal dedi-
catory epistle, Hamilton (the translator) described Count
de Pagan the author, as a "French earl of most ancient
nobility, and descent from the famous and honourable
commanders in the Holy warres, who for their wise conduct, and rare valour, were employed in places of great
trust, and transmitted them with their Crest of Arms and
name of Pagan, which was the badge of their great ex-
ploits in mating and killing the Pagans or infidels, to their
successors of the same name and family, as the Author
himself shows at large in the dedication of his rare book
of Fortifications, to another branch of the same family."

The work here referred to, "Pagan on Fortifications,"
was not to be found in any of the Scottish libraries, but I
got it in the British Museum. Since then Mr William
Downing Bruce of Lincoln's Inn, barrister-at-law, London, and recorder of Wallingford, has obliged me with
his copy of the same work, and which he holds in right
of his wife, Mrs Louisa Emily Plomer, only daughter of
Mr William Plomer, D.L., and Mrs Catherine Pagan, only

child and heiress of Mr William Pagan of Linburn, Linlithgow, and Picardy Place, Edinburgh — a gentleman, Glasgow by birth, but Dumfriesshire by extraction.

The title of the Fortifications (folio) is " Les Fortifications du comte de Pagan. A Paris M.DC.XLV. Avec privilege du Roy." The following is a transcript therefrom of the origin and rise and progress of his family, as given by Count de Pagan, embracing the long period of years from 980 to 1645, and stating the several authorities whence he gathered his facts :—

" DES ARMES DE LA MAISON DE PAGAN.

"Les Armes de la Maison de Pagan sont, bandé d'or et d'azur de six pieces au chef de Bretagne chargé d'vn Lambel de gueules ; a la bordure componee de France-Naples et de Hierusalem. Les six bandes d'or et d'azur, furent portees par les Anciens Seigneurs de cette famille en la Bretagne Armorique,* l'vn desquels nommé Albert prenant pourfemme la niepce du Duc de la mesme Prouince, prist aussi les Hermines en ses Armes : et passant les Alpes enuiron l'an 980, auec Tancred nepueu du Duc de Normandie, pour combatre les Sarrazins, fut le premier qui porta dans l'Italie les six bandes d'or et d'azur au Chef de Bretagne : lesquelles Armes furent ainsi gardees, par son fils Albertin surnommé de Pagan †.

* Filiberto Campanile dell insegne de' Nobili. Scipione Mazella, delle Famiglie illustri d'Italia, il Marchesi. Le Pere de Varennes Iesuite en son Roy d'Armes, page 338. Siluester petra sancta in Tesseris Gentilitiis, cap. 69, p. 595, &c.

† Albertino de' Pagani ; Albertin est diminutif d'Albert, selon l'vsage des Italiens, comme s'ils disoient, le ieune ou le petit Albert ; et Pagani est le nom qu'ils donnent aux Sarrazins et Infideles.

par les Italiẽs en 1010, pour auoir chassé les Infideles
Mahometans de la Campanie, et pris la Ville de Nocere
où ils s'estoient fortifiez depuis cent ans ; pendant que
les douze fils de Tancred les chassoiẽt de la Pouille et de
la Calabre. Par Sigisbert de Pagan qui en l'annee 1038,
passa en Sicile contre les mesmes Sarrazins, auec Guillaume
Duc de Calabre et Maniace general des Grecs. Par Pagan
de Pagan * lequel auec Emme sa femme se trouuoit Seigneur de la Forenza en Basilicate l'an 1084. Et par Iean de
Pagan,† dont les factions troublerent long-temps à Rome
le Pontificat du Pape Vrbain II. principalement aux annees
1095 et 1096 comme il est remarqué dans les Histoires.

"Le Lambel de gueules de trois pieces fut adiousté a ces
anciennes Armes l'an 1118. Par Huges de Pagan ‡
Fondateur et premier Grand Maistre de l'Ordre des
Tẽpliers en la Terre saincte ; honoré du tiltre d'Illustre
et de Noble Cheualier dans les Histoires, et Chef de
l'Ambassade enuoyee de la part du Roy Baudouyn II. et
des Chrestiẽs du Royaume de Hierusalem l'an 1128, au
Pape, à l'Empereur, aux Roys et aux Princes de la Chres
tienté pour auoir du secours, à la teste duquel, montant

---

* Pagano de' Pagani ; les mesmes Autheurs citent la donation
qu'il fist, des Eglises de saint Iean de Sala et de sainte Constantine,
à Berenger Abbé de la Trinité de Venose.

† Platina in vita Vrb. 2. dit, Verum mortuo Ioanne Pagane
seditiosissimo homine, &c. La traduction Italienne met seditiosissimo cittadino, mal a propos.

‡ Hugo de' Pagani, voyez Guill. Arch. Tirius, in Hist. sacra,
Card. Baronius, tom. 12. sub anno 1118. Giac. Bosio, tom. I.
dell' Hist. di Malta, Paul Emile ; Volaterran ; Pierre Messie,
Fauin ; Campanile, et autres infinis.

Il est dit, vir nobilis et venerabilis de ordine equestri, et fut
esleu Grand Maistre l'an 1127, par les suffrages de plus de 300
Cheualiers de son Ordre des meilleures maisons de l'Europe.

à plus de trente mille personnes de toutes conditions, il
repassa du port de Marseille en la Terre saincte. Passant
en France il obstint la confirmation de son Ordre du Con-
cile general de Troys en Champagne, et treuuant saint
Bernard en cette celebre Assemblee, il y reçeut de ses
propres mains des reigles pour ses Cheualiers Religieux.
Or ce Lambel de gueules estoit la deuise de ces genereux
Guerriers, voulās signifier par ce Rasteau rouge qu'ils
ramassoient la saincte terre par l'effusion de leur sang ;
et ce fut en ces voyages, que Charles d'Anjou * frere du
Roy saint Louis, prist ce mesme Lambel pour brisure en
ses Armes de France ; lequel fut aussi retenu par Didier de
Pagan frere de Hugues et par ses descendans, entre lesquels sont les plus remarquables, Iean de Pagan Protecteur de l'Ordre des Templiers en Italie l'an 1158.
Pagan de Pagan † Seigneur de la Forenza et Senechal du
Royaume de Naples en 1170, sous le Roy Guillaume II. de
la Race des Normās.   Abielard de Pagan Protecteur des
mesmes Tēpliers fōdez par ses Ancestres comme il se void
aussi dans les Archiues Royales de l'annee 1192. Guillaume de Pagan Seigneur de la Forenza, de Prata, de Sāto
Padre, de Lotino, de saint Iean Incarico, de Canta lupo,
de Gualdo, de santa Resta, de Buccone et de Casaluiero
en 1200.   Iean de Pagan Seigneur des mesmes terres que
son Pere, lequel en 1239, fut auec Guillaume son fils et
les autres Barons du Royaume, en la guerre de Lombardie
pour l'Empereur Frederic II. Roy de Naples. Iean de
Pagan Gouuerneur de la Ville de Cosence Capitale de la
Calabre, faict General de la Cauallerie du Royaume de

---

* Charles d'Aniou donna ces mesmes Armes au Royaume de
Naples enuiron l'an 1270.
   † Pagano de' Pagani et les suiuans, voyez les mesmes, Campa-
nile, Mazella et il Marchesi tous della Famiglia Pagana.

Naples en 1271, par Charles I. frere de saint Louis Roy
de Frāce. Thomas, Guillaume et Adinolphe de Pagan,
lesquels /apres la perte des batailles de Beneuent et de
saint Germain, et la mort des Roys Mafred et Conradin
eurent recours à la clemence de Charles d'Aniou, qui les
receut en sa Cour, les conserua dans leurs biens, et les
honora du tiltre de Nobles Cheualiers en 1270. Pierre de
Pagā * lequel sortir du Royaume de Naples par la diuision
des guerres, fut Chef du party des Gibellins en la Romagne, où il s'acquist par les Armes la possession de plu-
sieurs terres et Chasteaux, auec la fameuse forteresse de
Sosenane : Il se rendist aussi Maistre de la Ville d'Imole
sur les Bolonnois en 1263. Et la perdant il se remist
dans celle de Faenza où sa faction estoit la plus puissante.
Il est encore dit Gentil-homme de grande condition par
les Historiens, et venant à mourir, il laissa son ieune fils
Maynard sous la tutelle de la Republique de Florēce,
pour le garātir comme elle sit, de l'oppression de ses
Ennemis, les Cōtes Guidi,† les Vbaldins et autres grands
Seigneurs de la Romagne. Maynard de Pagā‡ dit de

* Pietro Pagana, voyez Car. Sigonius de Regno Italiæ, lib. 19.
Pompeo Vizani dell' Hist. di Bologna, lib. 3. Leandro Alberti,
della discrittione d'Italia, fol. 32. Campanile, Mazella et Iean
Villani Historien, page 286, ou il dit entr'autres choses, Piero
Pagano grande Gentilhuomo.

† Conti Guidi, d'ou les Marquis de Bagni selon Alberti et Sansouin.

‡ Mainardo Pagano ou Maghinardo da Susinnana. Voyez
Campanile. Mazella. Leonardo d'Arezzo en l'Hist. de Florence,
Pompeo Vizani Hist. di Bologna, lib. 4. Leā Villani, page 168, 275,
283, 286, 300, et 306. Leandro Alberti, f. 303, 312, 315, 316,
320, et 321. Francesco Zazzera della casa di Mōtefeltro. Landino
et Dante, Poetes, Ses Eloges en Villani sont Grāde et Sauio Tirāno.
Gran Signore in Romagna. Buon et Sauio Capitano di Guerra.
Benauenturoso in piu bataglie : Sauio fu di guerra, et in suo

Sosenane, General des Gibellins en Italie, Prince con-
querant des villes d'Imola, Cesena, Forli, Faenza, et de la
plus grãde partie de la Romagne, victorieux en diuerses
batailles, et non moins celebre par la beauté de son corps,
par la grandeur de son courage, et par sa Prudence à la
guerre, que par sa gratitude enuers les Florentins ses
Tuteurs, quoy que Guelphes.   En 1289, il se ioignit auec
eux, et se treuuant à la grande bataille donnee le II. de
Iuin dans le Casentin, la Victoire de son party donna
beaucoup d'esclat à sa gloire.   En 1290, il prist auec son
Armee la Ville de Faenza.   En 1291, il surprist celle de
Forli, et fit prisonnier le Comte Guidi de Romena frere
de l'Euesque. d'Arezze Gouuerneur pour le Pape, de la
Romagne.   En 1293, il adiousta la Ville de Cesne à ses
Conquestes.   En 1296, il fit ligue auec le Marquis de
Ferrare, et suiui des Alidoses, Manfredes et Ordelaphes,
du Comte de Montefeltre et du Tyran de Pise, il deffit en
bataille rangee le premier iour du mois d'Auril les Guelphes et les Bolõnois, et prist d'assaut la Ville d'Imole.
Et en 1299, il accorda genereusement. la Paix, que le
Cardinal Valerian Legat de Boniface VIII. et les Am-
bassadeurs de Florence Neri, et Brunelleschi negotierent,
enfin pour le repos de l'Italie.   Ce grand et sage Tyran,
ainsi lé nomment les Historiës, mourut dans sa gloire en
la Ville d'Imole l'an 1302, laissant son Estat à son
nepueu Louys Alidose de Pagan,* auquel l'Empereur

---

tempo fece grã cose; et autres choses fort magnifiques sur sa
recognoissance enuers les Florentins. Et Alberti, fol. 316, dit de
plus que Mainardo Pagano fu huomo di corpo bello et di virtu
militare egregio.
    * De Ludouico Alidosio cognominato Pagano, selon Fr. Sã-
souin delli signori d'Imola. Voyez Leandro Alberti, fol. 321, et
Nic Macchiauello, lib. I. delle Historie.

Louis de Bauiere donna le tiltre de Prince souuerain
d'Imola, où sa posterité regna l'espace de 120 ans et
iusques au temps d'vn autre Louis Alidose dernier Prince
de cette famille.   Anthoyne de Pagan * Seigneur de Prata,
lequel se rendant aupres du Roy Charles II. en 1289, auec
Hector del Tuffo son Beau pere et les autres Barons de la
Prouince du Principat pour la deffence du Royaume de
Naples ; fut seul honoré du tiltre de Dominus ou de
Seigneur, parmy tāt de noblesse.   Eustache de Pagan,
Conseiller et Ministre d'Estat du Roy Robert, General
de ses Armes en Achaye l'an 1316, Vice-Roy de la Prouince
de Calabre en 1321, et Mareschal du Royaume de Naples
en 1323, il eut encore en 1325 la commission d'assembler
et de mettre en ordre auec vn pouuoir general et absolu,
la grande Armee, que le mesme Roy Robert fist em-
barquer et passer en Sicile, sous la conduite de Charles
Duc de Calabre son fils.   Zarlin de Pagan, lequel se porta
auec tant de valeur en la guerre de Sicile de l'annee 1342,
qu'apres la prise de la Ville de Melasso il en eust le
Gouuernement du Roy Robert, et la confiscation des biens
de Lothaire Cygale ; Il fut encore honorablement em-
ployé dans les mesmes guerres par la Reyne Ieāne pre-
miere en 1343.   Thomas de Pagan,† Mareschal du
Royaume et grand Escuyer du Roy Charles III. en 1381,
lequel fut ennoyé dans les Prouinces de Barry, et de
Basilicate l'an 1382, auec ample pouuoir d'en fortifier les

---

* Anthonio Pagano et les suiuās; Voyez Filiberto Căpanile
dell'Insegne de' Nobili Scipione Mazella delle Famiglie illustri
d'Italia.   Il Marchesi et autres chroniqueš Italiennes, de familles
Illustres, citees par eux.

† Vir nobilis, Thomas Paganus miles, scuteriæ nostræ Magister
dilectus.   Ex Archiuis regiis, entr'autres remarques de ces
Autheurs.

places importantes, et d'y commander et ordonner toutes
choses pour la guerre. Il eust encore en 1386, le Gouuernement du Chasteau sainct Elme, Forteresse de la Ville
de Naples, pour luy et pour ses enfans masles à perpe-
tuité : et des l'année 1380, il se treuue interuenir à la
Cour, pour des affaires publiques, comme Gentil-homme
Neapolitain du Siege de Porto, duquel iouyssoit alors
et iouyt encore cette famille.* Et Nicolas de Pagan
Archeuesque de la Ville de Naples par la faueur du Roy
Ladislas, et par les Bulles du Pape Boniface IX. de
l'annee 1398.

"Quant à la Bordure composee de France-Naples, et de
Hierusalem, elle fut adioustee à ces Armes l'an 1398, par
la concession du Roy Louys II. donnee à Galeot de Pagan,†
et aux siens le premier du mois de Iuin, dans laquelle il
louë la Noblesse de son sang, le merite de ses Ancestres,
les bonnes Alliances par eux contractées, et autres choses
semblables. Or ce Galeot, Grand Maistre de la Maison du
Roy Ladislas, Seneschal du Royaume de Naples, Conseiller d'Estat du Roy Louis II., Gouuerneur des Chasteaux
importans de Naples, de Rhege et de Mataree, Heritier
des grãds biens de Martinel de Pagan son nepueu, mort en
1396 ; et Mary de Catherinelle de Constance fut le premier de sa Maison qui porta cette Illustre Bordure en
'Escu de ses Armes.‡ Lesquelles sont ainsi demeurees à
ses successeurs et à ceux de ceste famille, les plus appa-
rens desquels ont esté depuis Paduan de Pagan grand

* Voyez la descrittione del Regno di Napoli.

† Vir nobilis, Galeotus Paganus miles, castri nostri sancti Erasmi
Castellanus, &c., le reste de cette concession ce voit en partie dans
Companile, Mazella et autres, conforme aux Registres de la Chan-
cellerie de Naples de l'annee 1398.

‡ Les Armes de Naples sont d'azur semé de fleurs de lys d'or, au
Lambel en Chef de gueules et celles de Hierusalem d'argent à vne
Croix potencee d'or, cantonnee de quatre petites de mesme.

Escuyerd Alfonce premier, Roy de Naples, de Sicile,
d'Aragō et de Sardaigne en 1440, Thomas de Pagan
Grand Seneschal du Royaume de Naples, sous le Roy
Ferdinand premier en 1460.[*] Car depuis la venue des
Arragonnois en Italie, le tiltre de Grād fut adiousté à ce-
luy des premieres charges de ce Royaume. Charles de
Pagan Seigneur de Briscilian, Conseiller et Grand Cham-
bellan de la Reyne Isabelle de Clermont en 1459,[†] lequel
eut pour femme Catherinelle de Gennare sœur du Comte
de Martirauo. Galeot de Pagan Seigneur de la Vetrana,
de Sorbo, de Serpico, et de sancto Stefano en 1481,
Grand Escuyer d'Alphonce Duc de Calabre, depuis Roy
de Naples et Capitaine d'vne Compagnie de Gens-d'armes
eu la guerre d'Otrāte contre les Turcs. Pierre de Pagan,
General de l'Artillerie du Royaume de Naples, Conseiller
et Ministre d'Estat des Roys Ferdinand II. et Federic III.
Ambassadeur en Hongrie, à Milan, et à Florence, l'an
1489, et Vice-Roy de la Prouince du Principat en 1496.
Fabio, Thomas, Alphonce, et Mario de Pagan, lesquels
dans les Estats Generaux du Royaume de Naples, tenus
en l'annee 1516, incontinent apres la mort du Roy Ferdinand le Catholique, s'opposerent ouuertement à la recep-
tion de la Reyne Ieanne III. secondés seulement des
Seigneurs de la Maison de Constance.[‡] Iean Baptiste de
Pagan,[§] dont la Viuacité de l'Esprit, l'agreement de la

---

[*] De tous ceux-cy, voyez tousiours Cāpanile, Mazella et autres
chroniques des familles Illustres d'Italie.

[†] Des Comtes de Clermont en Daulphiné; selon Sansouin eu la
famille des Vrsins.

[‡] Pandolfo Collenuccio dell' Hist. di Napoli n'allegue en ce ren-
contre que les Seigneurs des familles Pagana et Constança fondez
sur la fatalité du nom des Reynes Ieannes, si funeste au Royaumes
de Naples.

[§] Hier. Cardanus in Genesi Baptistæ Pagan, figura 25, et Iuncti-
nus in speculo Astrologico sur Ptolomee, lib. 3, cap. 12.

personne et l'Histoire tragique de sa mort aduenue le vingt-sixiesme Iuillet 1526, se voyet ensemble dans les cent Genitures de Cardan.   Cæsar de Pagan, lequel choisi par l'Empereur Charles-Quint, pour commander les Volontaires de son Armee d'Affrique, fut tué en la bataille de Tunis l'an 1535, combattant vaillamment contre les Infideles.   Alphonce de Pagan, Seigneur de la Vetrane et autres lieux en 1560, qui eut pour femme Marie Cantelme, sœur du Duc de Popoli.   Mutio de Pagan* Colonel d'vn Regiment de Neapolitains dans les guerres de Lombardie, et Capitaine encore de deux Compagnies de Cauallerie en celles de Flandres, où ils passa l'an ·1573, auec le grand Prieur de Requescens, Gouuerneur de l'Estat de Milan ; et de rechef auec Don Iean d'Austriche en 1578, où sa valeur parut en diuerses occasions, notamment en la bataille de Gueblours, en laquelle toute l'Armee des Flamens sousleuez fut entierement deffaite par les mille cheuaux qu'il conduisoit en l'Auant garde de celle du Roy d'Espagne.†   Mais il iouit peu de sa gloire, car cet homme courageux, vaillant et fidele, ce sont les termes de l'Historien, fut tué dans Arescot dont il estoit Gouuerneur, en vne sedition des Rebelles la mesme annee 1578.   Charles de Pagan, Seigneur de la Vtrane, de Sorbe, de Serpico, et de saint Estienne en 1590, lequel eut pour femme Louyse de Mirabel sœur du Marquis de Briscigliano.   Ferdinand ou Ferrand de Pagan,‡ lequel enueloppé dans le tumulte

---

* Mutio Pagano, Voyez Campanile, Mazella ; le Card. Bentiuoglio, tom. I. des guerres de Flandres.   Famianus Strada I. Decade de l'Hist. de Flandres ; Emanuel de Meteren au grand Volume des guerres du Pays bas et autres.

† Viro forti fidoque, qui æger è Lecto ad tumultum accurrerat, interempto, le mesme Strada, lib. 10.

‡ Ferrante Pagano, accompagné de son frere Decio en son voyage de France.

de la Ville de Naples,* de l'an 1547, sortit enfin du Royaume en 1552, auec le Prince de Salerne, et les autres
Seigneurs Neapolitains, qui passoiët en France, pour ap-
peller Henry II. à la conqueste de Naples ; lequel approu-
uant ces propositions commençoit à se disposer à l'entre-
prise.† Mais ils perdirent bien-tost auec ce Roy l'Espe-
rance de leur retour à la Patrie, et treunans dans les
troubles de la France la ruine de leurs fortunes, ils eurent
diuers succés, car sans parler des autres, le Prince de Salerne mourut enfin Huguenot en Prouence dans vn village de peu de nom, et Cæsar Mormille fist en peu de
temps son raccommodement en Espagne. Quant à Ferrand de Pagan, il fut Cheualier de l'Ordre et Gentil-
homme de la Chambre du Roy et tonsiours honoré du
tiltre de Seigneur et qualifié Gentil homme Neapolitain,
dans les breuets‡ et lettres des Roys, Charles IX. en 1565,
Henry III. en 1576, et Henry quatriesme en 1592, de
mesme que dans les Registres de la Chamber Royalle des
Comtes de l'an 1576, au roole des Pensionnaires Italiens,
il fut encore Lieutenant de la Compagnie des Gens-d'
armes du Connestable Henry de Mont-morency, General
de la Cauallerie de son Armee du Languedoc, et Gouuerneur de la Ville et Chasteau de Beaucaire en la mesme
Prouince, et s'estant trouué dans Auignon l'an 1563, il
y fut declaré Chef des Armes du Pape, par le Vice-Legat,
pour s'opposer au Baron des Adrets General des Hugue-

* De ce tumulte, voyez le mesme Căpanile, nella Famiglia Sanseu-
erina et Iean Sleydan Historiē Aleman.

† Le Roy Henry qu'ils trouuerent à Thionuille ·selon le mesme
Sleydan et le sieur d'Aubigné Historien François.

‡ Ces Breuets sont de Bordeaux, de Paris, et du Siege de Rouen,
les deux derniers sont de milles escus de pension annuelle, verifiee
en la Chambre des Comptes de Paris.

nots et Victorieux des Catholiques, contre lequel sortant
auec la Noblesse de la Ville, les troupes Italiennes, et les
Compagnies du Païs, il le combattit au Pontet* auec tant
de valeur qu'il l'obligea de se retirer, cõme il fist, de la
Prouince d'Auignon. Il fut aussi Gouuerneur pour sa
saincteté du Chasteau et Baronnie du pont de Sorgues et
s'estant marié dans Auignon † auec Marie de Merle sœur du
Seigneur de Beauchamp, dont il n'eust pour fils que Claude
de Pagan ‡ mon Pere. Il y mourut enfin l'an 1607, pendant que le Duc de Sauoye demandoit son raccommodement en Espagne, par le seul motif de son affection,
l'ayant cogneu dans les guerres de Prouence. ·Et Cæsar
de Pagan § Seigneur de la Pietra et de Terranoua en 1600,
lequel ioigãt les sçiences à la noblesse, et la magnificence
aux richesses, composa dans l'oysiueté de la Paix, cette
belle et curieuse Histoire du Royaume de Naples qui
n'est point encore imprimee, et acheua son grand et mag-
nifique Palais accompagné d'vne place d'egale structure,
digne ornement de la belle Ville de Naples. Et ce fust

* De son combat du Pontet, voyez Louis de Perussis en son
Hist. des guerres du Comtat d'Auignon.

† De son mariage, ou de cette branche de la maison de Pagan
passee de Naples en Auignon, voyez Cæsar Nostradamus en son
Hist. de Prouence, et Morinus in Astronomia restituta, Parte 5,
pag. 119.

‡ Seigneur de Merueille et de l'Isle, de par sa femme Margue-
rite de Cocils en 1602. Gentil-hõme ordinaire de la Chambre du
Roy auec pension annuelle de 1200 escus, et Gouuerneur pour sa
Saincteté du Chasteau et Baronnie du Pont de Sorgues. Il mourut
à la Cour du Roy Louys XIII l'an 1620 au retour du voyage de
Bearn.

§ De Cæsare Pagano, voyez Filiberto Campanile nella Famiglia
Pagana et autres ; et del Ducato di Terranoua, voyez la description
du Royaume de Naples en Italien, et la Pere de Varennes en son
Roy d'Armes, page 338.

en sa faueur que le Roy d'Espagne honnora du tiltre de
Duché sa Ville de **Estranoue** dans la Prouince du Principat, possedé maintenant par les siens, lesquels sans doute
approuueront plustot mon zele que mon dessein, puis
qu'en l'espace de huict iours seulement, et sans autres
memoires que ceux des Liures imprimés, i'ay entrepris de
faire cet abregé des plus Illustres de leurs Ancestres.

"DE INSIGNI COMITIS PAGANI EDITIONE ODA.

Frontem Camœnæ cingite laureis.
 Ducem feracis Parthenopes Decus,
 Et stirpe Maiorum potentem
 Fert animus resonare cantu.
Per bella dudum, rebus in arduis,
 Actis Celebrem Dextera reddidit ;
 Nunc ipsa bellorum Magistris
 Otia dant documenta belli.
Hinc, Regularum tramite præuio
 Aggressus vrbes mœnia diruit,
 Turres premuntur, tota stridet
 Aggeribus glomerata tellus.
Illinc, tuetur mœnia Circino
 Dum castra stipant ordine milites,
 Hostes domantur, cincta vallis
 Arx trepidat, minitatque cladem.
Fortes creantur fortibus et bonis,
 Rectique cultus pectora roborant.
 Virtute functos more Patrum
 Verus honos sequitur per æuum.

       P. de Tieuloy Parpaille."

Count de Pagan in compiling the above instructive chapter of Pagan genealogy, and rescuing the name from its vulgarly supposed origin, laid all acknowledged Pagans under special obligations to him. The fulness and clearness of his narrative is an encouraging instance of success in the pursuit of family relationship, extending over many continuous generations.

Count de Pagan was born at Avignon in Provence, March 3, 1604. He took to the profession of a soldier at fourteen, in which he signalised himself. He lost his eyesight from the effects of a pistol shot in battle, and turned himself to the study of mathematics and fortifications. He published his work on the latter subject in 1645. In 1651 he published his geometrical theorems. In 1655 he published an account of the river Amazons, already mentioned, and, though blind, he drew the chart of that river, which is attached to the work. In 1657 he published the theory of the planets; and in 1658 his astronomical tables. He died at Paris, November 18, 1665, and was never married. He also made morality and politics his study, and may be said to have drawn his own character in his *Homme Heroique*. That branch of his family which removed from Naples to France in 1552 became extinct in his person. (Abridged from the English Encyclopædia, London, 1802.)

I know not in what era, or how or by whom, the name was carried to the British isles. It will be work for some future day, (and for some other pen,) to solve that problem. The oldest Scottish record noticed by me where the name appears is a charter by David Second to the Abbacy of Coldingham, in Berwickshire, dated at Peebles in 1126, where " Paganus de Braiosa " was one of the witnesses. (See Mr William Robertson's index of charters

K

p. 155.) That same volume also mentions a charter granted by the same Scottish monarch in favour of " Malcom Pagainson," keeper of the king's gardens in Edinburgh.

The name is to be found in the west of Scotland records for nearly three centuries back. My own descent is from the Galloway side of the Nith. My great grandfather James Pagan owned Terreglestown in Terregles parish, as his birthplace; his father, who was from Colvend parish, also in Galloway, farmed at Terreglestown; and in Terregles churchyard lie their ashes with those of my grandfather James Pagan of Curriestanes, of my father William Pagan, and of numerous other relatives—already, I believe, some seven generations of them in that burying-ground. My birth chanced at Kelwood, in the parish of Dumfries, where my father farmed for a few years at the beginning of this century, under the Queensberry family. Kelwood is on the Lochar, and adjoins Horseholm, widely known as the cradle (and the grave) of the first steam plough ever tried in Scotland. That was some thirty years ago, and the soil being soft— part of Lochar Moss—both engine and plough sank in it. Fortunately that powerful agricultural implement has had better success in the east of Scotland, where it keeps above ground, and does its work well.

CLAYTON, FIFESHIRE,
February 1865.

BALLANTYNE AND COMPANY, PRINTERS, EDINBURGH.